W9-DGJ-826

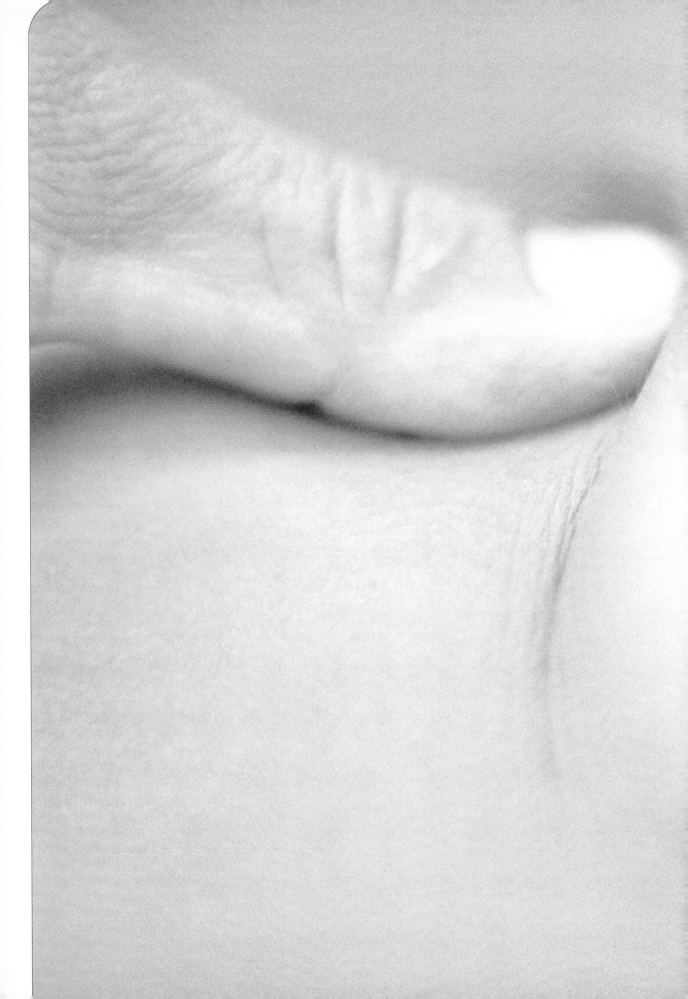

MASSAGE

BERNIE ROWEN

BARNES & NOBLE BOOKS
BOOKS
NEW YORK

Publisher: Mariëlle Renssen
Managing Editors: Claudia Dos Santos, Simon Pooley
Managing Art Editor: Richard MacArthur
Editor: Ingrid Corbett
Designer: Geraldine Cupido
Picture Research: Karla Kik, Bronwyn Allies
Illustrator: Alzette Prins
Production: Myrna Collins
Consultant: Chris Salvary

Reproduction by Hirt & Carter (Cape) Pty Ltd
Printed and bound in Malaysia by Times Offset (M) Sdn. Bhd

AUTHOR'S DEDICATION
This book is dedicated to my
husband, Ted, and my children
Brendon, Daryn, and Natali.

AUTHOR'S ACKNOWLEDGMENTS:

My thanks go to Hilda, for putting me in touch with the publishers; Ingrid Corbett, who has been an absolute delight to work with; Geraldine, for her insight in color coordination and design; Sandi from Serendipity Quintessentials for the loan of product for the photoshoot; Bubbles and Wendel for providing me with a silent retreat; and Heather for keeping my fingers on the keyboard.

C O N T E N T S

INTRODUCTION

WE HAVE ALL *bumped our knees at some time in our lives. Our first response? To rub them in order to ease the pain and make them feel better. Massage is the most natural form of healing, and one that many of us experience daily without giving it much thought; we may not even use the word massage to describe it. If your shoulders are sore, you may ask a friend to rub them; if your feet ache, you may take off your shoes and flex your toes; and which parent hasn't had to "rub it better" when a little one gets hurt?*

As we become increasingly self-sufficient and independent, human touch is becoming more difficult and to a large extent formalized. Massage is extremely nurturing and offers the means with which to break down the barriers we have set up around ourselves. It gives us the opportunity to reestablish natural human contact and benefit from a sense of relaxation and well-being.

A visitor to the East will often see, on a flat rooftop, a daughter in the process of massaging an elderly parent's shoulders—in many countries massage is recognized as not only being of great benefit, but also a way of life. There are often no formal schools or institutions to teach massage in these places, and the art is passed on by word of mouth or by means of drawings and diagrams.

This book teaches you how to massage using simple yet effective methods, and to embrace and understand a method of massage that is both useful and pleasurable. You will be taken through sequences that will provide the maximum benefit for your partner, but you will also be able to concentrate on just one section, such as massaging the back, and do this on its own. You do not need to be a massage therapist to enjoy the benefit of massage by using these methods at home, nor do you need to buy expensive equipment. If you can use your hands, you can achieve wonders.

Left **In the East, massage is a way of life— these women in Mongolia massage their children as part of a daily routine.**

THE HISTORY OF THERAPEUTIC MASSAGE

HEALING BY TOUCH has been practiced since man first walked the planet. Formal instruction in the use of massage as a healing tool was given in many countries as early as 5000 years ago. At Saqqara, in Egypt, this is evidenced by wall paintings in some of the ancient tombs: one picture executed in 2330BC depicts servants massaging the feet of a Pharaoh. In ancient Greece and Rome, physicians relied heavily on massage for the treatment and relief of pain—Julius Caesar, who suffered from neuralgia as a result of his epilepsy, was treated for severe headaches through the medium of massage.

In China the massage method known as *Tui na* was used in 2000BC during the dynasty of the Yellow Emperor. Subsequently, it continued to develop alongside the ancient art of acupuncture. The history of Ayurveda, the ancient Indian traditional medicine system that uses massage extensively as a part of treatment, was recorded over 5000 years ago.

Above **In Ayurvedic massage, which often forms part of a cleansing routine, the oils used are medicated or infused with various herbs. One method of application is to pour the oils onto the body while, or just before, rubbing the body.**

Between the years AD980 and 1037, Arab philosopher and physician Avicenna (Abu Ali ibn Sina) kept a most valuable record of medicinal plants relating to manipulation and massage. He was also one of the pioneers in the production of essential oils by distillation.

In Europe during the Middle Ages (fifth–11th centuries), both clergy and state stifled developments in many fields including medicine, and many records were kept clandestinely. There was a general scarcity of information, and records with regards to massage in particular were limited, since "matters of the flesh" were considered taboo. In the 18th century, surgery and allopathic medicine enjoyed increasing popularity, followed by the development of the manufacture of synthetic drugs. This in turn led to a situation where the public, and doctors in particular, became increasingly critical of natural methods of healing such as herbalism, massage, reflexology, and other popular alternative therapeutic practices known today.

Massage began to return to favor when Per Hendrik Ling opened the Central Institute of Gymnastics in Stockholm in 1813. Ling used his understanding of gymnastics, anatomy, and physiology together with the knowledge available from the Chinese, Greek, and Egyptian systems to develop what is currently known as Swedish Massage. Courses were run, and it in fact became the first modern formalized method of massage-technique teaching.

Subsequently, massage schools in the Western world have proliferated, and many different types of massage are taught. It is interesting to note that in the East there are very few institutions offering formal training in massage alone—massage is usually offered only as part of a course that deals with holistic medicine and therapy. In China there are facilities for traditional training in massage specially structured for blind women. They practice their massage strokes and finger exercises on bags of rice to strengthen their hands—a real challenge as it takes much time and willpower, not to mention the physical exertion that is required to crush the rice into a powder.

Left These hieroglyphs at Saqqara, Egypt, date from the Pharaonic period (c2345–2181BC) and depict a masseur tending the hand of a customer.

WHY MASSAGE?

AS TOUCH IS so natural, we do not all need to undergo formal courses to be able to give someone an effective massage. We experience an entire world through touch, and massage is only another aspect of this experience, albeit sometimes more concentrated.

We can distinguish between different textures just by touching them. Imagine a rough rock in your hand right now; think about what it would feel like. You will probably imagine it to be hard, cold, and very solid. You would probably not

think about lying or sleeping on it. Now, as a contrast, imagine a piece of silk—soft, pliable, slippery, and cool—and immediately you will conjure up thoughts of comfortable, perhaps even luxurious bed sheets. This is how we begin to understand how our ability to feel assists us in gathering information.

Have you ever put your hands on someone's shoulders and felt if they were tight or relaxed? Sometimes one can immediately feel a tensed bunch of muscles indicating tension or stress; one can often sense if the person is in pain; and one would certainly be able to feel if they were either hot or cold. When we are cold we often rub our hands together. This is so that we increase the blood flow to the area, and in so doing increase the temperature.

That therapeutic touch has a beneficial effect on the human body, and that the energy of caring is actually transferred, was proven many years ago. During World War II, experiments were carried out with infants in hospitals who were being treated for a wide variety of ailments—it was found that the infants who were picked up and cuddled gained weight more readily than those who were not; their health also improved more rapidly than those left in their cribs.

Above **Research carried out during World War II has shown that human touch can have a therapeutic effect on children.**

Massage Assists in Dealing with Stress

Stress in engineering terminology is defined as "the deformation or change caused on a body by the internal forces that work on it." The same definition can be applied to humans. Human beings are rather like elastic bands, in that they can be stretched only so far before they snap. The amount of stress we can take before we do snap is our stress limit.

A small amount of stress is good for us and produces adrenaline, which helps our bodies deal with emergencies. When primitive man lived in caves, he was continually surrounded by danger, exposed to the elements, and forced to survive by hunting wild animals, often large and dangerous. He suffered from stress occasioned by his circumstances and was constantly faced with the question: fight or flight? As a result of this situation the human body created its own protective mechanisms against stress. Our causes of stress may be very different to those of our ancestors, but they are constantly with us. In times of frustration, whether we are driving to the office during rush hour or hurrying to pick the children up from school, our body prepares itself for what could happen—the brain functions speed up into alert mode and chemical messengers known as hormones instruct the body to alter some of our operating systems. These are:

- The voluntary nervous system, which is the conscious system and the one that controls our voluntary actions, such as walking, picking things up, and holding a book.
- The involuntary or autonomic nervous system, which is the one that controls the functions of the body that do not require conscious thought, such as breathing.

Even though the threat to our lives is often imaginary, our body does not know how to differentiate between our imagination and the reality of the situation.

How does our memory work in regard to stress? Muscle fibers can in a sense be considered the body's memory banks when it comes to stress. Each and every membrane in the

> **The Body Responds to Stress by:**
> - Increasing our breathing rate.
> - Thickening our blood so that should we get cut, bitten, or otherwise injured, the clotting mechanism will be more effective.
> - Slowing down digestion as our body distributes energy to where it is most needed.
> - Increasing adrenaline output, which in turn causes the heart to beat faster.
> - Increasing our blood pressure.
> - Increasing metabolism of glucose, providing us with instant energy.

human body appears to have an unconscious memory that gets prodded on occasion, eliciting a familiar response. If we are experiencing a stressful situation, we seem to experience this stress physically in the body. The tight muscles in the shoulders are a result of too much stress. The hollow feeling in the pit of the stomach is a result of fear, which in turn results in stress. We often have to "harden" ourselves to deal with situations, and our muscles remember this and continually work to protect the body. Our inner dialog, which is never quiet, is essentially what creates our muscle tension.

THE BENEFITS OF MASSAGE

MASSAGE IS A pleasurable experience, and as such it assists the mind/body mechanisms to produce endorphins, which are the body's own natural pain relievers. Massage also:

- Normalizes blood pressure.
- Reduces the output of adrenaline.
- Assists to slow down rapid breathing.
- Reduces pain by relieving inflammation in the muscles.
- Increases circulation, which helps to bring nutrients to all the organs and the skin, thus promoting healing.
- Increases the flow of fluid throughout the body, which removes toxins.

Touch is one of the most pleasurable ways to relax our hardened muscles and allow the flow of life to course through our body again. When muscles are relaxed, all our physical processes show improvement and work more efficiently. We gain, or regain, a different perspective on life, as tense muscles and sluggish lymphatic systems tend to cloud our perception, offering a somewhat jaundiced perspective on life.

THE SKELETAL SYSTEM

Although one is inclined to think that the bones in the body are not affected by massage, this is not so. A tense muscle places the bone under substantial pressure or tension, as it is being "pulled" by the muscle. The ligaments that join the muscle to the bone are also tighter than they should be, and very little circulation can get to the bony structures because the capillaries and veins are contracted, much like a hosepipe when it is squeezed.

Our body needs all the oxygen it can get, and this is carried in the bloodstream through the veins, arteries, and capillaries. When massage takes place, the transportation of the necessary fluids is improved, either by removing toxins or by bringing fresh oxygenated blood to the body part that is being manipulated.

JOINTS

The skeletal system is made up of bones and joints. When the joints experience stiffness, it is usually due to overwork, or possibly injury, which causes toxins to collect in the joints, leading to arthritis or gout. The removal of these toxins by massaging the affected joint can bring much relief to the sufferer.

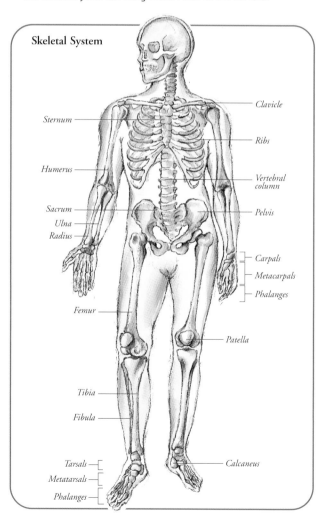

Skeletal System

Clavicle
Sternum
Ribs
Humerus
Vertebral column
Sacrum
Pelvis
Ulna
Radius
Carpals
Metacarpals
Phalanges
Femur
Patella
Tibia
Fibula
Tarsals
Metatarsals
Calcaneus
Phalanges

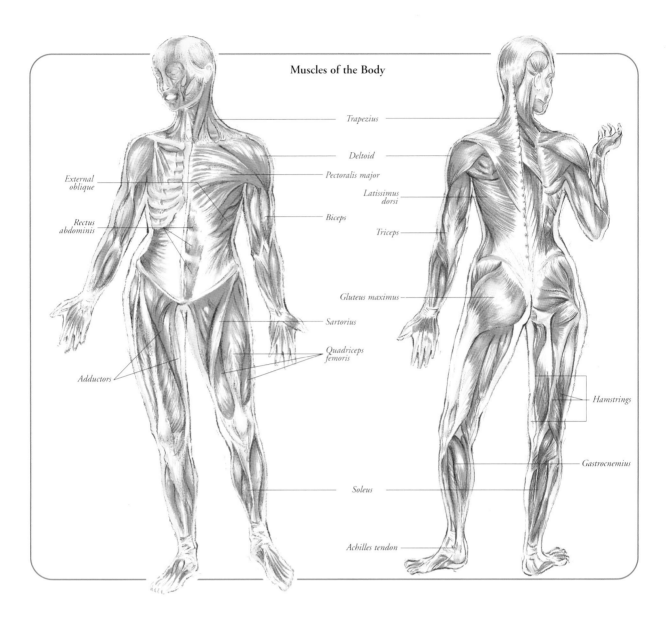

Muscles of the Body

Trapezius

Deltoid

Pectoralis major

External oblique

Latissimus dorsi

Rectus abdominis

Triceps

Biceps

Gluteus maximus

Sartorius

Quadriceps femoris

Adductors

Hamstrings

Gastrocnemius

Soleus

Achilles tendon

MUSCLES

The effects on the muscles are the most obvious in massage; this is where we really get results. Think back to the rock exercise described earlier in this chapter—remember the difference between the sensation of the rock and the silk? This is essentially how we see the difference between tense muscles before and after a massage.

Muscles also act as shock absorbers around our bones and joints. While the actual muscles are unlikely to suffer serious injury during day-to-day activities, they can become strained or damaged due to overuse, especially after strenuous exercise. Several hours after exercise, individuals may experience a condition known as delayed onset muscle soreness. This is essentially a manifestation of pain due to microtears in the muscle tissue. The muscle undergoes a biological process necessary for the repair and regeneration of muscle fibers, which brings with it a natural inflammatory response. Water retention associated with this inflammation puts pressure on sensitive pain receptors in the muscle. Massage assists in relieving this pain by moving fluid through the body, and thereby relieving water retention in the muscle tissue. Massage may also assist in reducing inflammation before it becomes extreme and dangerous.

THE RIGHT ENVIRONMENT

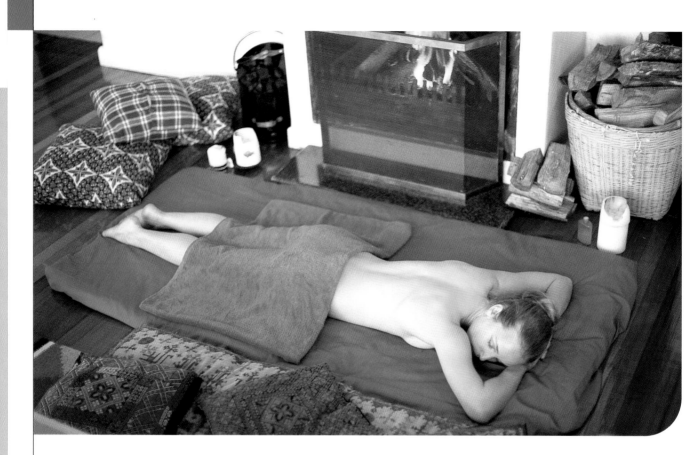

THE SURROUNDINGS ARE important when you are going to massage someone. One does not need a lot of equipment or a special room, however. All that is required is a comfortable, warm, quiet environment, with relaxing music; in warmer climates a quiet private garden is also a good choice.

Small rooms reflect intimacy, while medium-sized rooms encourage friendliness, i.e. massaging in front of a sitting-room fireplace would be considered friendly, but massaging in the bedroom would be considered intimate. Bear this in mind when massaging a partner or friend. It really depends on the relationship that you have with the person as to the most appropriate place to do the massage.

The most important considerations are: no clutter, no children playing and running around, no telephone to interrupt you, and a generally relaxing atmosphere.

A few of the basics you will need include:

- ☐ A blanket to lie on if you are working on the floor.
- ☐ Bath towels or blankets to cover the person being massaged.
- ☐ Massage oil.
- ☐ Gentle music (optional).
- ☐ Subdued lighting.

Above **A relaxing massage can be given with great effect in the cozy surroundings of a warm living room.**

Music

Your collection of CDs or tapes should include music suitable for playing during a massage. It should be tranquil and gentle. Music with vocals exercises the mind of the listener, and can conjure up memories that may be unwanted or painful. This could partially negate the benefits of massage that act on physical, emotional, and mental aspects. Whale sounds are good, as

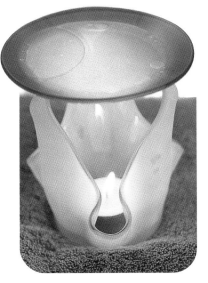

well as the sound of streams and rivers with gentle birdsong. This type of music will help your partner to relax completely.

Candles and Fragrant Oils

A lit candle assists in creating the right atmosphere, and has the effect of dissipating negative energy.

You should also consider the use of an oil burner with some soft fragrance to assist relaxation and establish the right ambience for the massage.

Oil burners come in many shapes and sizes and generally consist of a ceramic container about 5–6in (12–16cm) high. A night light or food-warmer candle fits under a small bowl that rests at the top of the burner stand, and this is filled with water and three or four drops of essential oil. As the water and oil mixture heats up, the oil evaporates and diffuses into the air, giving off the fragrance of the oil.

When using essential oils in a treatment, it is wise to ensure that the fragrance on the burner is similar to the one used in the sequence. The massage oil mixture should be prepared in advance and should be at room temperature.

Total Relaxation

In the East it is believed that if the head of the person being massaged is pointing south or east, the subject becomes more receptive to the massage, and a greater degree of relaxation is achieved.

If you decide on candlelight and soft music, and you ensure that the room is warm at all times, you have a good chance that the person being massaged will relax, sometimes to the extent of falling asleep! Recent studies indicate that sleep patterns may be disturbed where there is a river or main water supply running under the building, or power cables under the floor. If it is feasible to do the massage somewhere else, make the choice not to do it in a potential negative-stress area.

If you can place a small water fountain and an ionizer in the room so much the better, as this encourages positive energy and helps the masseur stay focused.

OUTDOORS

If the weather allows, it is a wonderful idea to do massage under trees near a burbling stream. Those of you who have an opportunity to do this should take it, as it is most liberating—natural surroundings create one of the best possible atmospheres for massage. Do remember that the person being massaged should be kept warm at all times.

TACT

Finally, you should be aware that there are certain mental and emotional qualities worth cultivating as a masseur. When receiving a massage, one of the greatest fears that recipients may have is that their bodies offend you. If they are overweight they may believe that an overweight body is unattractive. Alternatively, they may have a complex about being very thin.

Although you as the masseur realize that these complexes are unnecessary, you should be sensitive in this regard, as it will make the difference between the recipient being happy about the massage or enduring it because they feel that they "have to."

Above **You won't need music if you can massage outdoors—the sounds of nature provide the perfect background for relaxation.**

THE EFFECT OF COLOR

EACH DIFFERENT COLOR has its own energy frequency whose vibrations are able to affect the human body's own subtle energy vibrations. If you are going to use colored towels and blankets, here are some suggestions for creating a suitable atmosphere:

If your partner has sore muscles, then **violet** is a good color to use. Violet is known to relax the muscles and is used in color healing as an antibiotic.

Indigo reduces swelling and pain, and firms the skin.

Blue is said to help with fevers and encourages healing sleep.

Green has peaceful and calming effects on the body and the mind.

Yellow stimulates the mind and should be avoided or used sparingly in the massage area, as the aim is to relax both the mind and body.

Having said that, in the case of very tight muscles, **lemon** yellow in the area may well help. This is a color for the mind, so if you want to enhance intellectual stimulation, use at least a yellow towel for the head area.

Orange is an invigorating color and is used to promote confidence.

Red is very invigorating, and if you need to stimulate the circulation and warm the person that you are massaging, then it can be quite a fun color to use. Note that it will certainly not cause relaxation. Where a person requires detoxifying, the use of red is appropriate, as increasing the circulation assists in detoxifying the body.

Pink is the color of love, so if your partner is also your lover, then choose this wonderful color for your surroundings.

Having said all this, don't limit yourself to these colors. Use what comes to hand and that which you can easily access. If you do massage on a regular basis, however, you may want to have a special set of towels and blankets for the right occasion.

HAND EXERCISES FOR THE MASSEUR

WHEN STARTING TO massage, you may find that your hands get tired quite quickly. One of the best remedies for this is to strengthen your hands and fingers by doing a few simple exercises:

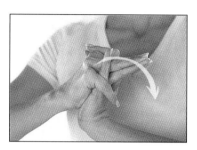

1. *Get a small rubber ball—a squash ball is excellent for this purpose—and squeeze it. Keep it on your desk at work or in your pocket and use it often. Apart from strengthening your hands, this exercise is also a magnificent stress reliever.*

2. *Hold your hands out in front of you and stretch your fingers out as far as you can, then make your hand into a fist. Extending your fingers in this manner will assist in strengthening them and bring increased circulation to the hands. While your hands are in a fist, rotate your wrist clockwise and then counterclockwise.*

3. *Hook your hands together, palms facing each other and fingers gripping the tops of the opposite hand. Stretch the index fingers up against each other and gently push the left-hand index finger against the right-hand index finger, so that it flexes slightly backward. Repeat the motion in the other direction. Continue with the rest of your fingers until you have done all of them individually. Then do the whole hand.*

4. *"Play the piano" by drumming your fingers on a tabletop or other hard surface. Starting with the thumb, move to the index finger, middle finger, ring finger, and little finger. Then reverse the motion, starting with the little finger, ring finger, middle finger, index finger, then thumb. Allow for flexibility and see how fast you can do this, as it will greatly assist in hand and finger coordination.*

5. *Put your hands into the prayer position and push them together, making sure that you make total contact with the palm surfaces.*

6. *Shake your fingers vigorously, making sure that your wrists are relaxed, so that you get rid of all the tension in your hands and increase the circulation. Allow the fingers to be so relaxed that they flick against each other, without you being in control of the movement. You should only control your elbow and wrist.*

RELAXATION EXERCISES FOR THE MASSEUR

WHEN MASSAGING A partner, you may spend a long period of time on the floor, bent over, or kneeling at a low level. In order for you to remain relaxed while doing the massage, you may wish to do some back and shoulder exercises before getting started. Tension will interrupt the massage flow; your partner will sense this and also become tense, defeating the object of the whole exercise.

The following exercises are geared to assist you to unwind, so that the recipient gets the maximum benefit from your own relaxed state:

1. Sit on a chair and pull your stomach in. Keeping your spine straight, breathe in deeply, ensuring that you are breathing right into the lower part of your lungs. Exhale for the count of five. Breathe in again for the count of six. Then exhale, doing this slowly so as to increase relaxation.

2. Rotate your left shoulder. Relax on the in-breath, and while breathing out through your mouth, push your shoulder forward, then up to your ear, and then toward the back. This will automatically assist in relaxing your shoulders. Do this with each shoulder separately and then with both together. Remember breathing.

3. Point your chin slightly down to ease neck tension, but don't touch the chest. Breathe in for the count of three while raising your shoulders toward your ears. Then, on breathing out, drop the shoulders rapidly. This exercise will also relax the shoulders.

4. Breathe in for the count of three, and at the same time stretch your arms up above your head, clasp your hands together, and stretch toward the sky. On your out-breath, slowly bring your hands down to your sides.

5. Sit on a chair, place your legs apart, and breathe in for the count of five. Stretch your back and lift your arms above your head. Gently drop your head onto your chest, keeping your arms raised. Then lower your arms between your legs to the floor, so that your back gently curves forward. Gently stretch your arms past your feet and lower your chest onto your knees while breathing out. Work to your own capacity. This is not a competition; it is designed to relax you.

6. Sit up slowly and stretch your feet in front of you. Rotate your ankles, first the right foot and then the left. This is a simple exercise, but it does wonders for abdominal muscles.

BACK STRENGTHENING EXERCISES FOR THE MASSEUR

THERE ARE A number of back exercises designed for the masseur that will assist in preventing back injury while working on the floor.

1. Lie on your back. Bend your knees toward your body and breathe in for the count of five. On the out-breath, keeping your legs bent, lower them sideways to the left-hand side of your body, keeping both shoulders on the floor and one foot directly on top of the other. You will feel a gentle stretch in your lower back. Breathe in and repeat the exercise on the left-hand side.

2. Still lying on your back, breathe in, lift your right knee halfway toward your body, breathe out, and bring your knee to your chest, gently squeezing the lower abdomen and stretching the lower back by lifting your head to meet the knee. You can help yourself by gently pulling the knee to your chest with your hands, but don't overdo this stretch. While breathing in, put the foot back on the floor, keeping your knee bent. Repeat this with the left knee.

3. Get onto your hands and knees in a crawling position. Breathe in for the count of five, keeping your spine straight and head dropped slightly. While breathing out, exhale through your mouth, arch your back, hang your head down, then come back to the resting position and breathe in. Exhale and lower your stomach toward the floor, bending your back the opposite way while lifting your head.

After completing these exercises, lie on your right-hand side with your right leg straight and left leg bent slightly; your right knee can rest on a cushion. Breathe easily and rest for a few moments.

This combination of exercise and relaxation will strengthen your body and relax your mind. A weary or unfit masseuse can transfer tiredness to the recipient, and tension can easily be detected in your touch, negating the benefits of massage.

> **Please note:** if you have any physical ailment, consult your health practitioner before doing any of these exercises.

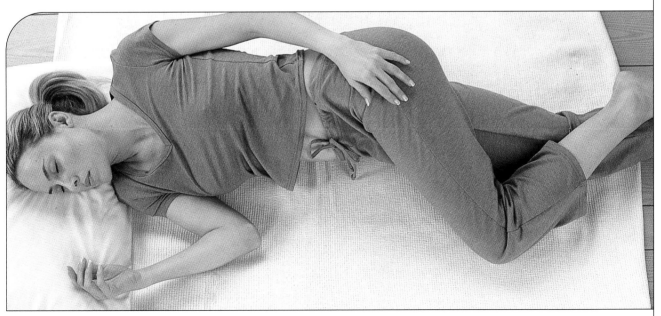

To GIVE AN *effective massage and work the muscles of the body with ease, you will want to make use of the appropriate oils.*

Carrier oils such as sunflower and olive oil are found in most kitchens and are indeed suitable for massage. However, there are many oils that can also be beneficial to the skin, such as grapeseed oil and almond oil.

While carrier oils assist the smooth gliding of your hands, essential oils such as lavender and chamomile will lend the massage a more pleasant and therapeutic effect. This chapter offers an overview of various types of oils and their properties, as well as "recipes" suitable for a variety of situations and circumstances.

Right **There is a wonderful variety of herbs and essential oil extracts that can be combined with carrier oils for the perfect massage medium.**

MASSAGE OILS

OUR MUSCLES respond so warmly to touch, that every stroke used in massage will have a different effect on the body.

This chapter will introduce the soothing and basic connecting stroke known as effleurage; the lifting and squeezing action of petrissage, which assists the muscle fibers to stretch; tapotement, which sensitizes the nerves; and thumb strokes, often used to reach deeper tissue.

You will also become familiar with kneading, useful for massaging over large muscle areas, such as the thigh and back, and feathering, which works on a more subtle level and is best used at the end of a sequence of strokes.

An understanding of these strokes will allow you to put together an effective and relaxing massage sequence.

Right **If you are short on time, a good option is to concentrate your efforts on a back massage.**

The Basic Strokes

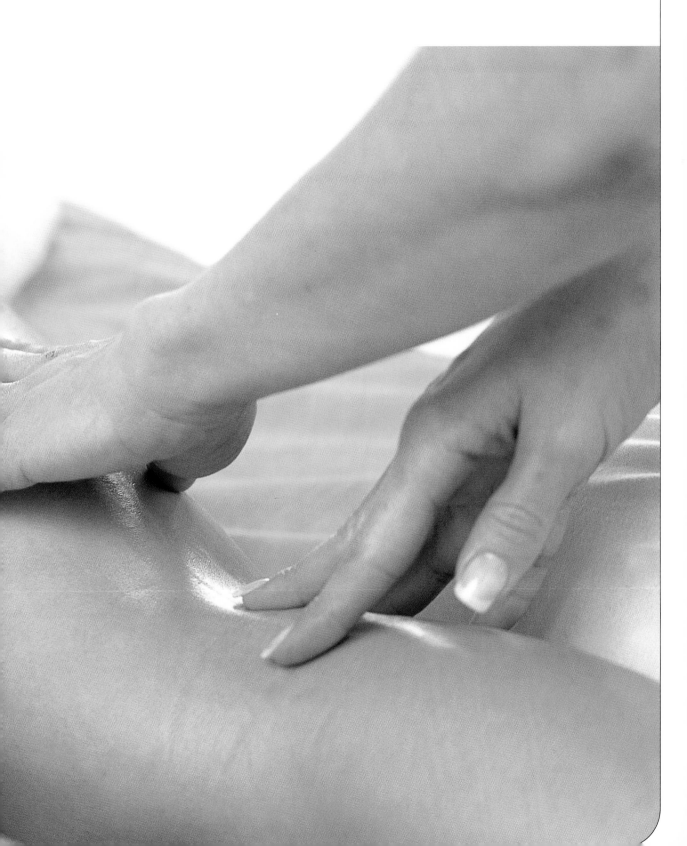

EFFLEURAGE

EFFLEURAGE IS A gentle, gliding stroke, and as such can be considered one of the most important relaxation techniques in massage. The sliding effect of this method smoothes and soothes, and can also be used as a connecting stroke to fill in between the different movements or types of strokes that will be used during the massage sequence.

1 *Use effleurage strokes to begin the massage; a good way to start is with a light sliding motion in the direction of the heart. You must allow the recipient's muscles to fit snugly in your hand.*

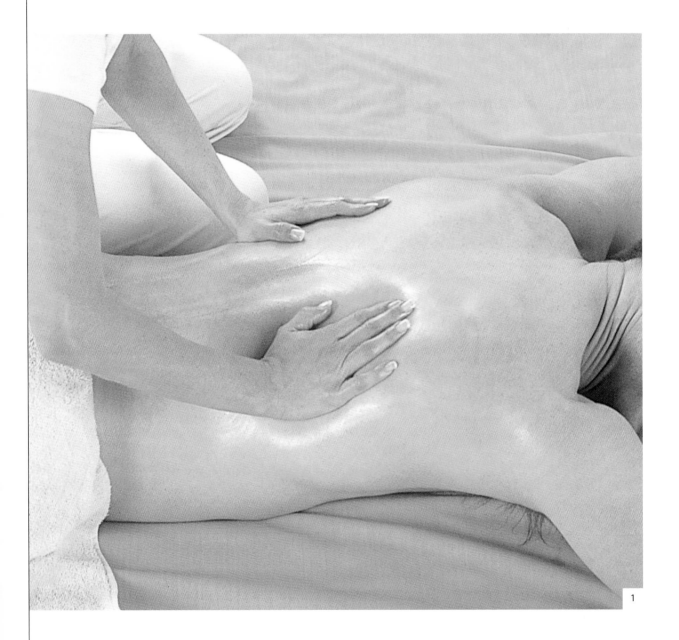

1

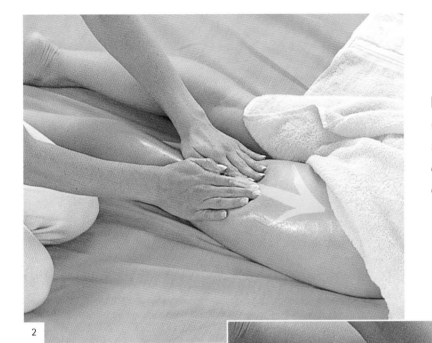

2 *Apply medium pressure with your whole hand, gliding smoothly along the length of the muscle. This stroke will assist in spreading the oil over the skin and will initiate relaxation.*

3 *Once the muscles are sufficiently relaxed, you can use slightly deeper sliding, or slightly increased pressure of the hands over the same area. Remember to use body weight to apply pressure, and keep your back and arms relatively straight to avoid backache and tiring too quickly.*

Effleurage is the means by which you apply oil to the body. This stroke is the perfect method to begin a massage, as it allows the other person to become familiar with your hands. It can also be used as a long stroke on the legs and as a circular motion on the larger areas such as the back. In this instance, effleurage lends itself to the use of gliding circles over the whole area.

The long, gliding stroke of effleurage is fluid in movement, much like a gentle flow of water over rocks; it increases the familiarity between your hands and the recipient's body, promoting the relationship of trust that you wish to establish during massage. This technique is also the manner in which you slide your hands off the body after a massage routine, almost as though to leave behind a memory of the strokes.

PETRISSAGE

PETRISSAGE IS A gentle pinching movement that increases circulation and brings the blood toward the small capillaries in the skin. It is done with alternate hands working in sequence, one after the other, on the more fleshy areas of the body such as the thigh and buttock area. This method of squeezing may also be described as kneading, but you would not in this instance push down on the body.

It is often not possible to wrap the hand around the whole muscle when doing petrissage; whenever you are working on a larger muscle area, lift parts of the muscle and then squeeze lightly, though still firmly enough to have a gentle grip on it. This technique helps to release toxins into the bloodstream, in turn facilitating their excretion. Petrissage, therefore, is healing to muscle fibers.

1 *Take your fingers and gently grasp and squeeze a handful of flesh, keeping your fingers quite straight so that you are in fact pulling a bit of flesh, then release it and repeat the same procedure slightly further along, using the other hand.*

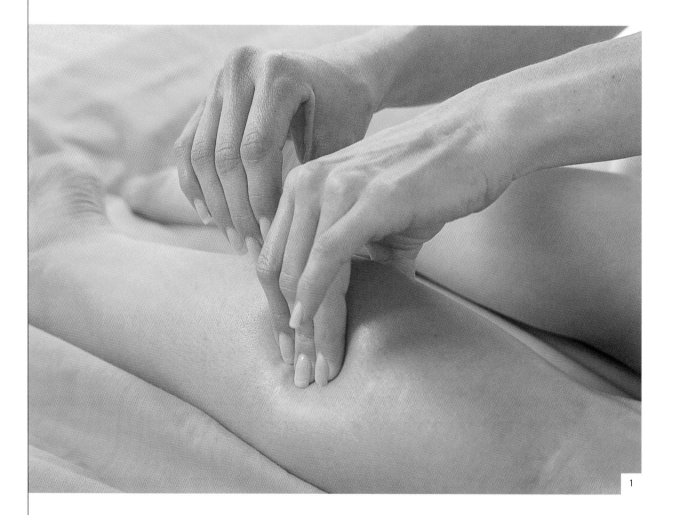

1

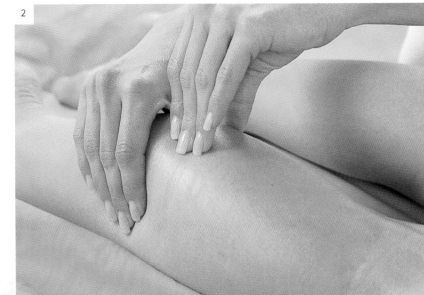

2

2 *Move gently and rhythmically along the limb or area being massaged, ensuring as always that you work up the body toward the heart.*

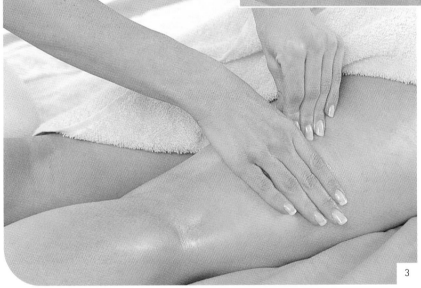

3

3 *Over the large muscles, such as the hamstrings, your hands should stretch out quite substantially so as to be able to grip a greater portion of the leg—this will ensure that you do not pinch the muscle.*

The key to an effective petrissage stroke is to do it with the same pressure throughout the massage, rhythmically and slowly. Strokes that are slow and rhythmic are the most relaxing for both giver and recipient, which is an important aspect of massage.

Petrissage also encourages the removal of excess fluid from the muscles. After strenuous exercise, muscle tissue can become damaged; this damage brings with it inflammation and water retention, which put pressure on the pain receptors in the muscle (see p17). When massaging the legs to relieve this pain, you would first use the gliding strokes described in effleurage, then gentle petrissage pinching.

When working on arms and legs, petrissage is often used in conjunction with effleurage. On broader areas of the body, such as the back and chest, the muscles are flat and more difficult to grasp, and in these instances it is recommended that kneading or thumb strokes be used, plus a little tapotement to increase the circulation.

TAPOTEMENT

TAPOTEMENT IS A stimulating stroke and should be used only when you are doing a refreshing, invigorating massage. It is not part of the relaxing massage sequence. It is a useful stroke to know and practice, however, as the person being massaged may on a particular occasion need to be stimulated rather than relaxed.

The tapotement technique is used to improve the supply of blood to the area being worked on, and can be used before certain types of exercise, e.g. where explosive power is needed.

The first method of tapotement, and the least vigorous, is to gently and rapidly patter the fingers onto the body like falling raindrops, alternating fingers individually as though drumming on a table. In traditional massage there are other strokes that fall into the category of tapotement, such as cupping, where the hands are partially closed like a cup and then gently slapped onto the recipient's body.

Tapotement and cupping strokes stimulate soft tissue areas. The speed and percussion of these vigorous movements encourage the flow of blood to the skin and stimulate nerve endings; as such they are not generally included in a relaxing massage sequence.

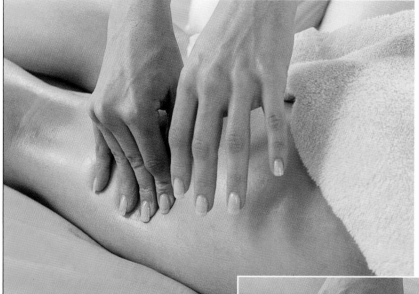

1

1 + 2 *With your fingers slightly spread apart, rest your fingertips against the skin. Lift your wrists and move your hands up and down, drumming your fingers quite firmly against the skin, in a similar movement to one you might make in a straight line across a keyboard.*

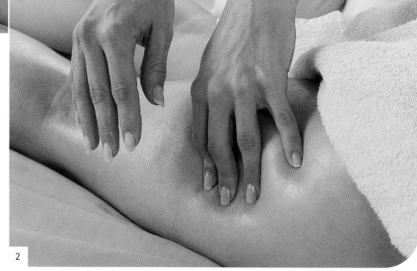

2

FEATHERING

FEATHERING IS WHEN you allow your fingers to lightly brush over the skin using alternate hands, keeping them relaxed so that a similar energy can be transmitted from you to the recipient without too much effort. Care must be taken that feathering does not tickle, so you should use slightly firm but light strokes. Many individuals are very sensitive to a light touch, and tickling can easily irritate and bring about annoyance rather than relaxation.

Practice feathering on your own leg first and see what it feels like. It should have the effect of relaxing and not stimulating the muscle.

Feathering is an extremely gentle and relaxing stroke often used to join other strokes in sequence. If you have allowed your hands to glide up the leg using an effleurage stroke, then you can feather your fingers back down to the foot. A good way in which to end a treatment is by feathering from the knee down toward the ankle—a technique that is almost guaranteed to make the recipient fall asleep!

Falling asleep immediately after or during a massage should be regarded as a compliment by the masseur, as massage is all about extreme relaxation.

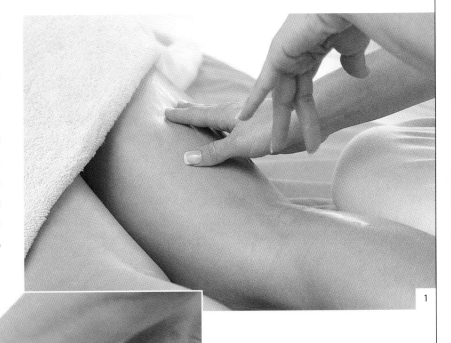

1

2

1 + 2 *Very lightly touch the skin with the tips of your fingers, stroking down the muscle with alternating hands.*

Start the movement of the second hand almost where you left off with the first, slowly moving down the limb that you are working on.

CIRCLING AND STROKING

THUMB CIRCLING

This stroke consists of using both thumbs and rotating them over a muscle to relieve tension. Try the following experiment: put one thumb on top of the middle of your thigh, at a midpoint between your knee and groin. Using small circular motions, rotate your thumb. The fingers of your hand are supporting the thumb by giving gentle support to the other side of the leg. Now try to feel the different textures under your thumb. In some areas your muscles may feel quite firm, in others softer, and the movement of the thumb may be painful. If so, then see what it feels like with less pressure. Do you need to lighten up a bit? What happens when you move your hand faster? Slower? Harder? Softer? Lighter? Heavier? Be conscious of how these techniques feel, since when you massage someone else, he or she will experience the same feelings and the result will be either pleasure or pain.

Do frequent thumb circling on yourself, firstly to check the sensation, secondly to relieve your own muscle stress, and thirdly to strengthen your thumbs.

Thumb circling is used frequently on tight, sore muscles. As many people store stress in their shoulder muscles, the use of thumb circling on this area is invaluable. However, the thumb can be used in any of the areas that are difficult to reach, such as around joints, in the neck, and the inside of the elbow, where larger strokes are not as effective.

When starting to do massage, most people feel that their thumbs become tired very quickly. Should this happen to you then it is a good idea to frequently change the stroke back to the gliding effleurage technique. Do practice, however, because thumb circling is a wonderful experience for the person being massaged, especially when done up the back.

1 + 2 *Holding your thumbs apart from the rest of the hand, push down with the ball of your thumb and slide in a circular motion, releasing the pressure slightly as you come full circle. Repeat the stroke a thumb's width from the previous starting point.*

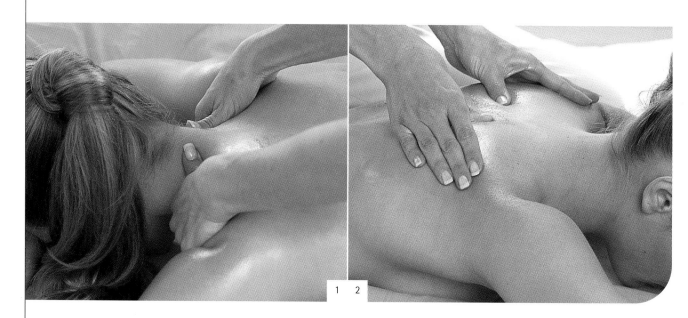

1   2

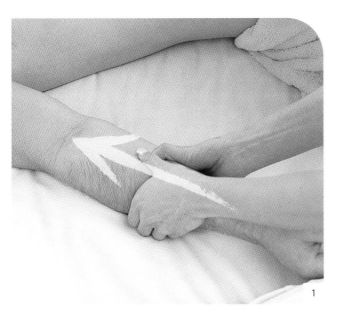

Thumb Strokes

Your thumbs, and thumb pads in particular, are excellent tools for locating specific areas of tension in the muscles, and for soothing out the knots that build up as a result of this tension.

Thumb strokes are effective on the neck and shoulders, hands, soles of the feet, and the face, and are often used in conjunction with thumb circling, with more pressure applied in the stroke than in the circling. On the face, it is simply a stroke without any real pressure.

1 *With your fingers kept curled into the palms of your hands, use your thumbs to stroke an area of tension in a long, gliding motion. This method is often used when working along a central "seam" on the arm or leg, or down the sides of the spine, where it serves to stimulate the nerves that radiate from the spinal cord.*

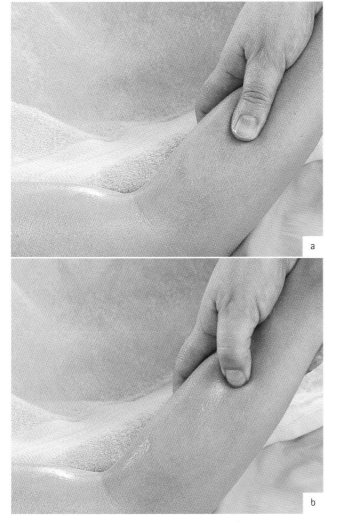

Thumb Crawling

This stroke involves using a crawling motion of the thumb in a manner similar to the way in which a caterpillar moves across a leaf—in fact, the stroke is often referred to as the "caterpillar crawl." Use your thumb to "walk" across an area, with a steady rhythm of pressure and slip, repeating the stroke until the entire area has been covered. This movement is particularly effective on the top of the foot.

a *Hold the limb with your fingers, stretching the thumb until it is resting on the area that you are going to work.*
b *Press the thumb firmly into the muscle, release, lift the thumb slightly, and press down again, covering the entire area in this way.*

LARGE CIRCLES

LARGE CIRCLES INVOLVE using the whole hand, with the pressure coming mainly from the heel of the hand —palm and finger giving support—moving in large circles.

This stroke is used mainly over large areas such as the back, and is both soothing and comforting. You can use large circles to move from one area of the back to another, and as it is a slow movement it is often helpful while you are deciding on the next sequence; the friction will keep the muscles warm, and contact with the person will not be interrupted.

Large circles on the back, as the name implies, are large, smooth, circular motions carried out from the base of the back, where the hands meet with thumbs resting on the *ilium* (the large bone at the base of the spine that spreads across the lower back and becomes the hip). Be very careful whenever working on the back that too much pressure is not applied over the spinal column. This is a golden rule in all types and movements of massage.

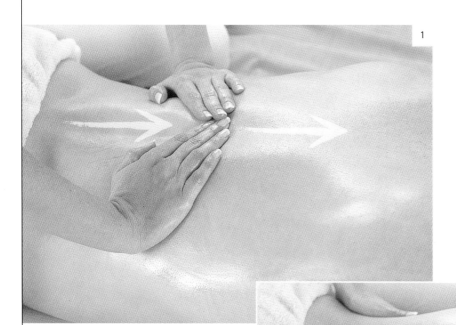

1

1️⃣ *Start with the hands facing the head, and then let them glide smoothly over the waist and come back in a circular motion, ending just a little higher than where the previous movement started.*

2️⃣ *Repeat this until you have reached the shoulders, making sure each time that you reach the sides of the body. This type of massage is used to cover large areas of the body reasonably quickly.*

2

WRINGING

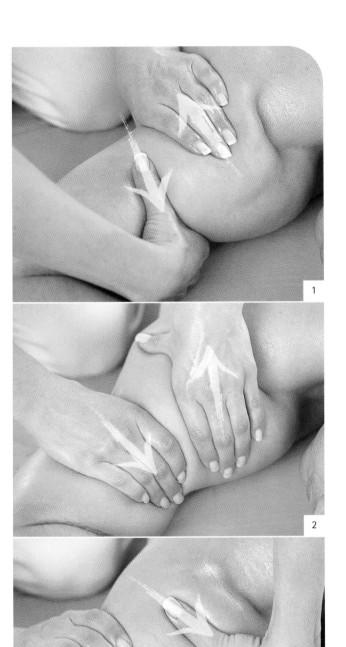

WRINGING HELPS TO move toxins out of the muscles and into the bloodstream, which in turn takes toxins through the organs of elimination, including the skin, lungs, kidneys, bladder, and bowels.

Wringing is used mainly on the arms, legs, and back. Allow your hands to completely cover the area that you choose to work on, then pull with each hand very lightly in opposite directions. If you are working on the arm, place your hands around the muscle and push with one hand, while pulling in the opposite direction with the other. At the midpoint of this movement, your hands should pass each other so that they can reach the opposite side of the limb. This stroke is repeated over the entire area, moving up a little way each time a stroke or movement is completed.

It is necessary to move slowly and rhythmically with each wringing stroke so that toxins are not trapped in the muscles. To ensure that the friction is not uncomfortable, be sure to use enough lubrication.

Never use wringing over joints and never use it on children, the elderly, or very thin people, as this can be damaging to delicate muscle fiber.

1 *Grasp the muscle at the shoulder between your cupped hands. Slide one hand away from you, squeezing firmly, and slide the other hand toward you in the same manner.*
2 *Your hands should pass each other and reach the opposite side of the arm.*
3 *Move down the length of the muscle using this wringing motion.*

KNEADING

KNEADING IS AN EFFECTIVE MOVEMENT or stroke used over large areas of muscle, such as in the thighs and buttocks, and involves the use of your fists. Make a fist and then move each finger individually as though you were drumming your fingers on the table, only using your knuckles. Fist kneading is quite a firm stroke, so be sure that the recipient is comfortable and does not suffer discomfort or pain while having it done. Try it on yourself in the first instance so you can judge just how much pressure to use. While seated, make a fist, put your curled-up fingers on your thigh, and move your fingers individually quite quickly along your thigh muscle. Feel how your muscles respond to the sensation. The friction caused generates warmth, which in turn leads to relaxation of the muscle—the object of the exercise.

1 *Make loose fists with your hands, ensuring that the middle section of your finger touches the skin. Push quite firmly into the muscle at the back of the thigh, moving your fingers from index to small finger with a light crawling action.*

Work over a small area in a circular motion and then move further down the muscle.

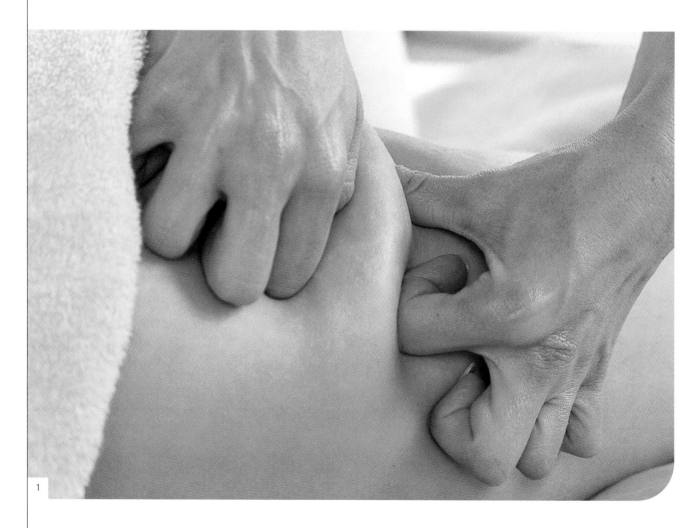

1

Deep Tissue Massage

Deep Tissue Massage is a term used mainly by individuals who administer sports massage, and is a good description of its purpose and function as it is used primarily on sportsmen and women for the relief of muscle pain. Deep tissue massage involves a fair amount of friction and uses the heel of the hand and the thumbs and fingers, working into the area where deeper tensions lie.

While a large number of athletes are known to strain their muscles due to strenuous training and performance, debili-tating stress can also be stored in the deeper layers of our muscle tissue, causing soreness. Deep tissue massage is an art, because the masseur has to exert enough pressure to cure the problem, but not cause discomfort or make the massage an unpleasant experience. If you get this combination right, it can bring great relief to someone with muscle sore-ness and stiffness, and helps to relieve pain.

Deep tissue massage strokes include a thumb-rolling technique that involves pressing one thumb into the flesh, sliding it up the muscle or area being massaged, then following it with the other thumb. You can do short thumb strokes, alternating with each thumb quite quickly so as to pick up a speedy rhythm. This is both invigorating and relaxing, but practice is needed to dis-cover the correct pressure. Once again, try it on yourself first to see how it feels.

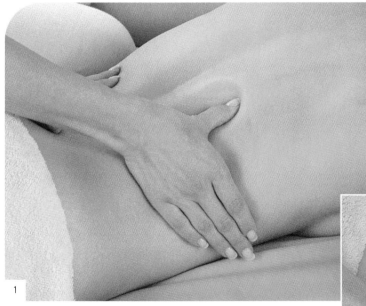

1

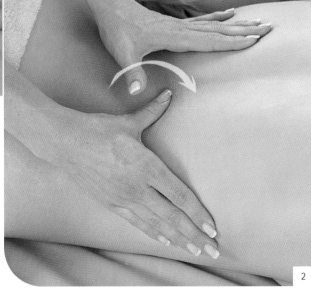

2

1 *For deep tissue work, alternate between your thumbs and the heel of your hands to press down into the muscle, and then firmly stroke along the area that you are working on.*

2 *When using the thumb-rolling technique, press one thumb firmly into the flesh, slide, then do the same with the other thumb, starting just above where you left off with the first thumb. You roll one thumb over the over in order to get back into position—hence the "rolling technique."*

HEEL OF THE HAND

THE HEEL OF the hand stroke is used when it is necessary to work over a large area of the body. It is usually confined to working on areas such as the back and thighs.

This stroke is effective for moving fluid through the body, which in turn encourages lymphatic drainage, one of the most important reasons for massage (*see* p19). The heel of the hand stroke also stimulates circulation and thus increases the uptake of oxygen. The increased supply of oxygen to the cells brings clarity to both body and mind, encouraging an overall sense of well-being.

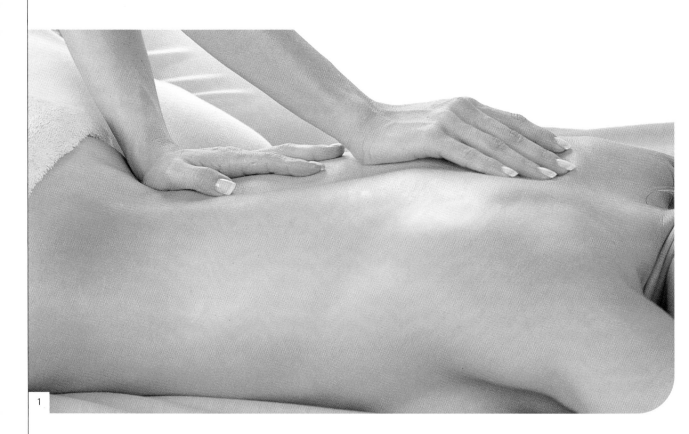

1

Straight to the Heart

All massage strokes are aimed at improving circulation, and therefore as a general rule should be toward the heart rather than away from it. Improved circulation stimulates the lymphatic system and assists in removing toxins from the muscles and cells. These toxins are filtered by the lymph nodes to prevent infection spreading into the bloodstream.

1 *Put pressure on the body with the heel of the hand and slide up the muscle, keeping the fingers in touch with the skin. The added sensation of fingers sliding over the body will serve as a gentle introduction to the firmer stroke.*

VIBRATION

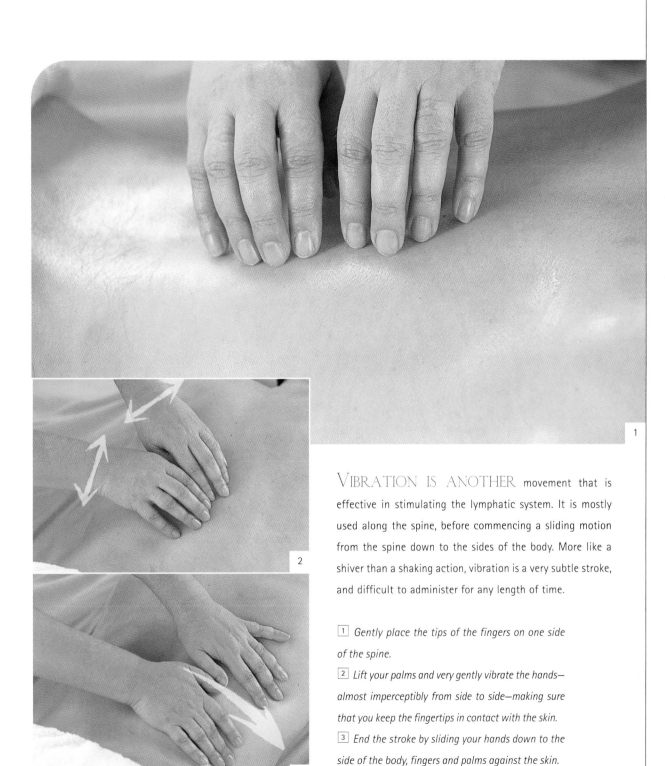

VIBRATION IS ANOTHER movement that is effective in stimulating the lymphatic system. It is mostly used along the spine, before commencing a sliding motion from the spine down to the sides of the body. More like a shiver than a shaking action, vibration is a very subtle stroke, and difficult to administer for any length of time.

1 *Gently place the tips of the fingers on one side of the spine.*

2 *Lift your palms and very gently vibrate the hands— almost imperceptibly from side to side—making sure that you keep the fingertips in contact with the skin.*

3 *End the stroke by sliding your hands down to the side of the body, fingers and palms against the skin.*

To ensure that *you will give an effective massage, it is important that you first understand and practice each movement separately. Once you are comfortable with individual strokes and techniques, you can bring a full massage together by practicing an existing sequence.*

There are just as many massage sequences as there are masseuses, however; so do not feel bound to adopt any rigid pattern or routine and stick to it forever. When you have learned your separate sequences on the different parts of the body, you can put them together any way you like, but in the beginning it helps to learn a sequence off by heart so that it becomes second nature to you, and you are confident that you enjoy giving a massage as much as the recipient enjoys receiving it.

Right **The head massage can often be the most relaxing part of the entire massage sequence.**

THE MASSAGE SEQUENCE

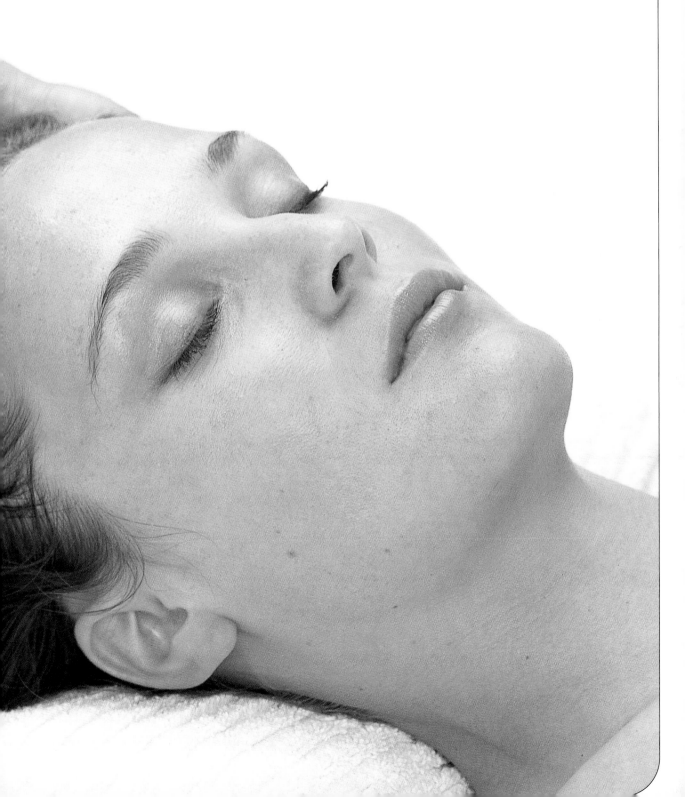

Getting Started

The floor is probably a good option to work on in the first instance. If you experience back problems yourself, it is advisable to use a massage plinth, or even have the recipient lie on a dining-room table. This may seem odd, but it eliminates the need for you to bend, stoop, or kneel. You should also enjoy the experience of giving a massage, and having a sore back as a result of doing this is no joy.

If kneeling on the floor, pay attention to yourself and your own comfort—this is of great importance, as the recipient of the massage will notice if you are not comfortable.

Start off by putting a comforter on the floor. Take a second comforter and lay it down, so that approximately one-third of the longest side overlaps the first one in a slightly offset position, top and bottom. This will result in a raised strip on which the recipient can lie, and a thinner strip on either side and at each end on which you, the masseuse, can kneel.

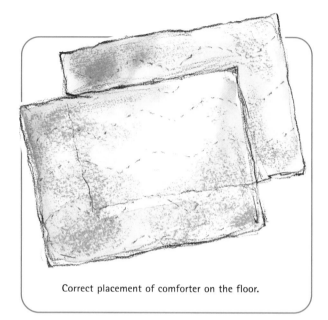

Correct placement of comforter on the floor.

It is recommended that you lay a plastic sheet over the quilts and cover this with a bath sheet, as it is inevitable that at some stage, however experienced you may be, you will knock over a bottle or container of oil.

For this same reason it is advisable that you use a plastic bottle with a narrow neck, so that knocking over the bottle does not become a tragedy and your quilts are not damaged.

Essential oils should not be kept in plastic containers while in their concentrated state, but once mixed with a carrier oil, the use of plastic bottles is customary.

Towels and Blankets

The relationship you have with your partner will determine whether he or she is entirely unclothed during the massage, or whether underwear is worn. You will in any event need two bath sheets, one to place underneath your partner and one to cover him or her. You will also need two bath towels and two small hand towels, one of which will come in handy if you want to cover the hair while massaging the face.

The DON'Ts of massage

It is important that the masseuse have short fingernails and that both the masseuse and the recipient remove all jewelry. There are also a number of contraindications for massage that should be emphasized.

You should not massage:

- over recent scar tissue.
- over varicose veins.
- over boils, skin infections, or rashes.
- anyone with athlete's foot, unless you keep well away from the feet. Athlete's foot is contagious, and a change of bath sheets, etc., will be necessary.
- when someone has a fever.
- when someone has cardiovascular disorders.
- when someone has phlebitis or thrombosis.

ATTITUDE

The attitude of the masseuse is of prime importance. You must be in a relaxed state of mind. Once you are in the right frame of mind, check the physical massage situation. You should have created the right atmosphere with the correct colors and music. The answering machine should be on, and the room should be warm and dimly lit, preferably with an oil burner emitting a relaxing fragrance. Allow yourself at least an hour-and-a-half for a full body massage. Having said that, don't set too strict a time frame—if you only have one hour, you will be able to do most of the massage, and if you only have half an hour, it is still better to do a back massage than nothing at all.

ENSURING COMFORT

Cover the recipient with a warm bath sheet, and make sure that he or she is comfortable. You may want to place a rolled-up towel under the knees, as this takes the pressure off the lower back and can ease any discomfort in this area. A cushion may be needed under the head.

It is well worth spending a minute or two before starting the massage to ensure that the recipient is feeling comfortable. If the massage starts with discomfort, it will end with discomfort.

Arrange for your partner to lie on his or her back. If you are working on the floor, kneel facing the feet. If you are working on a table, then stand facing the feet.

MAKING CONSCIOUS CONTACT

Gently rest your hands on the top of the foot, with your palms touching the top and your fingertips resting on the fold where the foot bends at the ankle. Relax your mind. Listen to the music for a moment. Let your hands feel the energy of your partner's body.

The bath sheet covering your partner can now be folded back to expose the portion of the leg as far as the knee. Grip one foot with your right hand by holding at the ankle. Then, with your left hand over the top of the foot and your right hand supporting the heel, pull the foot toward you very gently. Repeat this movement twice on each foot.

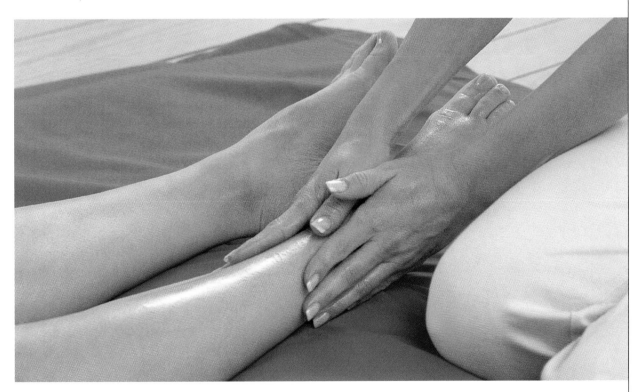

The Foot

Applying Oil

Take your hands off the feet and pour your oil mixture into the palm of one hand, then rub the oil into both hands, taking care not to use too much. Apply the oil to the feet in such a way that it is spread evenly and covers each foot entirely. If you are using powder or cornstarch instead of oil, then shake a little on your hands and follow the same procedure.

Ball of Foot Stretch

Make a fist with one hand and, holding the top of one foot in the palm of the other hand, gently push your fist into the ball of the foot [a]. This stretches the foot in a way that is seldom experienced in day-to-day movement. Don't be too gentle—the foot has to bear its owner's body weight and is quite strong—in this instance rather err on the side of force than caution. Ask the person being massaged how she feels, and she will soon tell you if you are being too hard on her. People have been put off massage after experiencing one that was too harsh.

Working the Instep

Put both your thumbs on the sole of the left foot on the inner side, with your fingers on top of the foot; then wring the foot in tiny sections, your hands moving in opposite directions [b]. Follow this with the other foot.

Top of the Foot

Work up the "valleys" between the bones of the upper foot from the base of the toes to the middle of the foot where the arch becomes visible, working away from yourself with the thumb-crawling movement known as the caterpillar crawl [c]. When you come to the bony part on the top of the foot, slide your thumb up to the ankle, and then slide the thumb back down into the next valley between the toes.

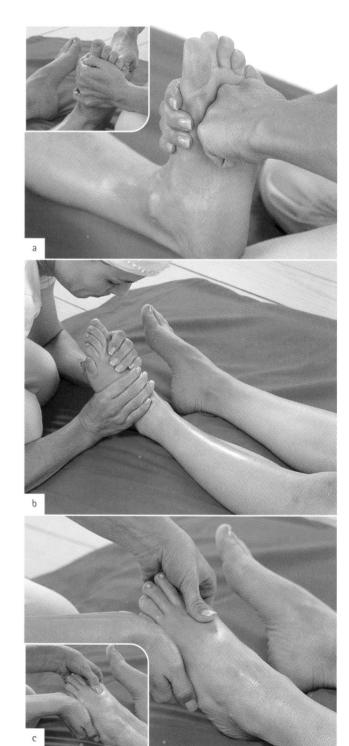

a

b

c

TOE TUG

When you have finished with the top of the foot, take each toe individually and tug it gently toward you 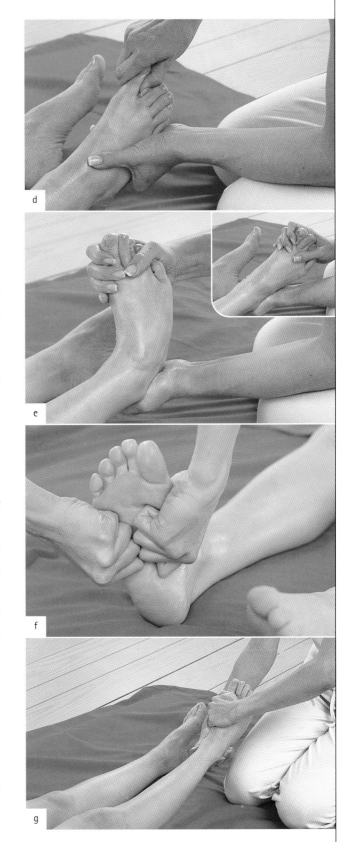d. Follow this with the toe twiddle.

TOE TWIDDLE

Taking each toe in turn rotate it ever so gently, first clockwise then counterclockwise, at the same time pulling on it very lightly.

FOOT ROTATIONS

Lightly grasp the top of one foot around the toes and, supporting the ankle with your other hand, rotate the entire foot e. Some people undergoing massage will have a natural inclination to do this movement for themselves. Try and get them to relax the foot and ankle so that you can rotate it for them, but don't insist. Spending too much time on a "tug-of-war" here will distract from the overall objective of the massage.

FOOT STRETCH

Put your fingers in the center of the foot on the longitudinal midline, with your palms near the outside edge of the foot f. Stretch the foot very gently over the knuckles while exerting a little pressure from the fingertips. Repeat this twice for each foot. This stretches the foot in a way that it seldom experiences with normal use. It is known as the most relaxing movement in the foot sequence, as it opens the chest and heart meridians and allows the energy to flow easily in these areas (*see* p90 on Reflexology).

PULLING THE FOOT

Taking the ankle in one hand, and supporting the heel in the other, pull the foot gently but firmly toward you g, repeating this twice for each foot. At this stage it is advisable to fold the bath sheet in-between the legs, covering the groin area to avoid embarrassment.

d

e

f

g

THE LEG

MOVING UP THE LEG

Having finished with the feet, apply more oil to your hands. Slide your hands up the left leg using the motion to apply oil smoothly to the skin. Use effleurage strokes, aiming the fingers of the right hand toward the inside of the leg and the left-hand fingers toward the outside of the leg, and slide your hands up as far as the knee. Gently separate the hands, slide the fingers around the kneecap, and then slide the hands back toward the foot in a light feathering movement. Repeat this rhythmically about seven times on each leg.

Next move to the right-hand side of your partner so that you are sitting facing the lower leg, and apply more oil if necessary. With your fingers cupping the calf muscle, rotate your thumbs gently up the outer sides of the shin [a]. When you reach the knee, slide your thumbs around the kneecap [b], cross them over each other briefly, then slide around the kneecap again and back down toward the ankle.

We appear to unconsciously retain a certain amount of stress in our muscles. Now is the time in the massage process to assure the involuntary nervous system that you can be trusted. Your partner might tell you that he trusts you, and really mean it, but the involuntary nervous system has to get used to your touch, and the first few strokes make all the difference to how the recipient enjoys the whole massage.

THE UPPER PART OF THE LEG

With your fingers directed toward each other, slide the palms of your hands up the top of the thigh, and then bring the hands back down the side of the thigh to the knee, with your thumbs along the top of the muscle. Slide the hands to just above the knee. Repeat this movement seven times on each leg, pulling slightly with the tips of your fingers as you move down the outside of the legs [c].

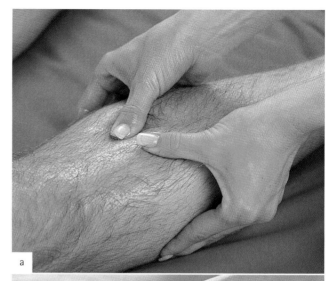
a

b

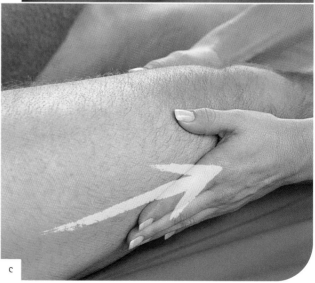
c

THE INNER THIGH

Bend the leg upward and place your left hand above the knee. Support the leg with the other hand. Slide your hand from the inside of the knee, up along the inner thigh all the way to the groin using a gentle effleurage stroke 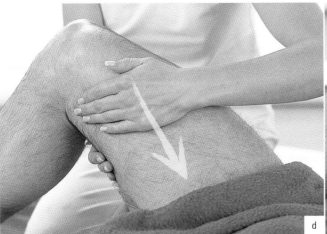. Repeat this motion, feathering back toward the knee on the down stroke. Again, using gentle pressure, stroke toward the groin. This movement assists in draining lymphatic fluid through the lymph nodes in the groin. When working toward the groin, bear in mind that this may be a sensitive area and treat the person being massaged with respect 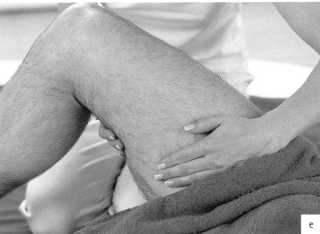.

d

e

MASSAGING THE CALF

A convenient time to massage the calf is when the leg is in the bent position. Taking the flat of the hand, glide it from the ankle up toward the back of the knee 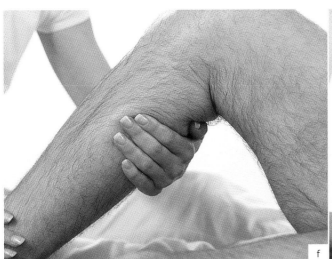. Making use of one hand, then the other, create a rhythm by bringing one hand up to the back of the knee, following immediately with the other hand 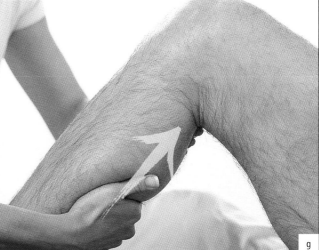. Repeat this at least seven times on the right leg. Move to the other side of the body and carry out the same procedure on the other leg. Again, repeat this seven times. Gently bring the legs back to a lying position with your partner still on his back.

f

g

Hand and Arm Massage

ALMOST EVERYTHING WE do involves our hands and arms, and as such these are probably the most overworked parts of our body. Like the feet, our hands contain a large number of sensory nerve endings and have many points that can be addressed by reflexology. A hand massage is therefore one of the most liberating and relaxing treatments that can be given, as it gently soothes and eases the nerve endings.

Hand Massage

Put some oil into your cupped hand and then rub it into the recipient's hands. Turn the hands so that the palms face upward. Slip one little finger between the recipient's ring finger and little finger, the other between the thumb and index finger ☐1, then stretch the recipient's fingers very gently, causing the palm to open. Having done this, massage the center of the palm with both your thumbs, gently rubbing over the center of the palm and toward the wrist ☐2.

Next, turn the recipient's hand palm down. Taking one finger at a time, hold it quite firmly and tug twice, gently, without cracking the knuckles ☐3 + ☐4. When tugging the finger, let your own thumb and forefinger slip off the tip of the fingers and then give your hand a little flick. This removes any possible negative energy that has accumulated in your fingers and can also serve to relax your hands.

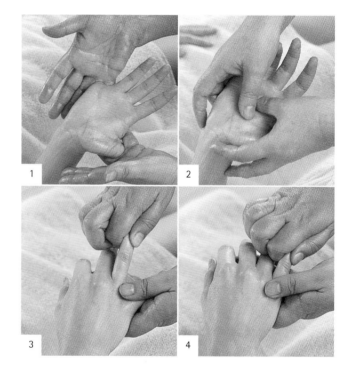

1 2

3 4

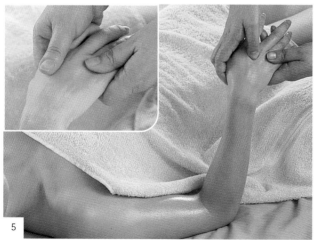

5

The Top of the Hands

You can now do the caterpillar crawl between the bones of the upper surface of the hand using thumb crawling. Gently allow your thumb to crawl up the valleys of the bones of the hand to the wrist, then slide your thumbs back down to the base of the fingers and let them glide to the next valley ☐5.

Next, place your palms on either side of the arm, close to the wrist. Move your hand up and down quite quickly and allow the recipient's hand to shake from side to side—this will encourage total hand relaxation.

MASSAGING THE ARM

Supporting the arm with one hand under the elbow, apply oil and spread it over the entire arm, from where it joins the shoulder to the wrist. If you are kneeling on the floor while massaging, you can support the recipient's arm on your leg. With your supporting fingers facing inward, glide the palm of your hand up the arm to the elbow, then bring your hand back toward the wrist by feathering down the sides of the arm. [a]

THE LYMPH DRAINAGE MOVEMENT

Very gently, with the flat of your hand, your little finger facing the inside of your partner's elbow, glide your hand down toward the inside crease of the elbow. Lymph nodes are situated here, and these will benefit from a gentle massage. Repeat this movement at least three times on each arm. [b]

Next, with a smooth motion gently lift the arm and continue to glide your hand on the inside of the arm right up to the armpit, feathering lightly on your way back to the wrist. Do this movement three times for each arm.

THUMB STROKES FOR THE ARM

Lie your partner's arm on the towel and wrap your hand around the arm so that your thumbs rest on the inside. Imagine that there is a seam up the center of the arm and, with your thumbs sliding up this "seam" [c], squeeze the muscle gently until you reach the elbow. Spread the thumbs across the crease of the elbow and feather down [d].

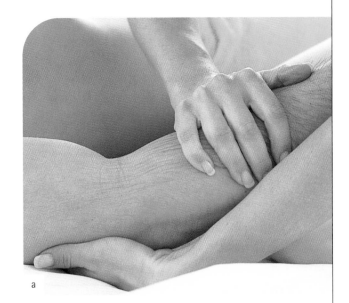

a

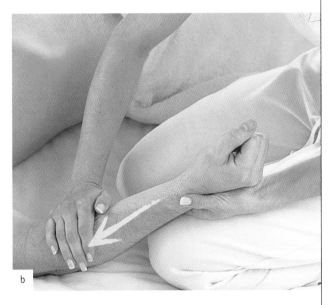

b

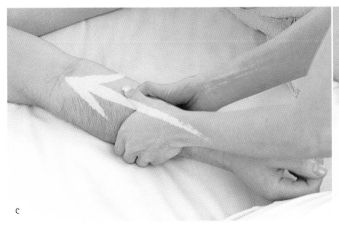

c

d

Upper Arm Massage

The deltoid muscles (shoulder) and the biceps (upper arm) often hold tension, and in people who do manual work or work out with weights, they are particularly well developed. This may present difficulties when working on these muscles, and more pressure than normal may be required. Don't over-do it, however, and check with the recipient to make sure that the pressure you are applying is comfortable.

The wringing movement [a] is appropriate here, as it works in opposition to the way in which the muscle fiber works (contraction and extension) and so relieves a fair amount of tension. Place your outermost hand just above the recipient's elbow, with your fingers on the inside of the arm. Place your other hand slightly higher on the arm; your hands should be holding, or cupping, the muscle. "Push" away from the body with one hand and "pull" toward you with the other in a wringing motion. Repeat this movement up the whole arm until you reach the shoulder. Do three repetitions of this movement.

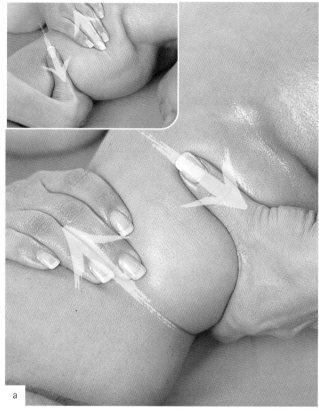

a

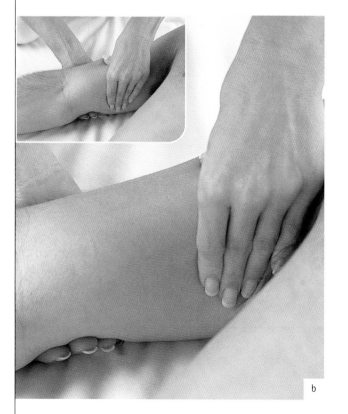

b

Thumb Circles on the Outer Arm

Rest the arm of the recipient on the towel. Support the elbow in one hand, and with the other cup your fingers around the inner arm with your thumb on the outer arm. Circle your thumb up the arm until you reach the shoulder [b]. You will feel the sensitive areas of the muscles. If you feel a knotty area, gently circle this with your thumb using moderate pressure until you feel the muscle relax. Gently feather all the way down from the shoulder to the fingertips. Do three repetitions of this movement.

Getting to the Other Arm

Slide your hands across the top of the chest so as not to break contact, and apply oil to the other arm. Repeat the aforementioned thumb circle sequence three times.

THE HEAD MASSAGE

AS YOU HAVE worked your way up the body, you are in a position to start working on the head. As the brain is the control center for our constantly overactive minds, a head massage is regarded by many people as a real treat and the highlight of the massage routine. This is the only massage area to which we do not apply oil.

The transition stroke to the head is done by sliding the hands toward the throat, being careful not to apply any pressure on the throat itself. Slide the fingers over the collar bone and around the top of the shoulders and down toward the back of the neck. Pause for a moment with your fingers on either side of the spine. This is a one-off movement with no repetition.

Place a rolled up towel under the neck so that the head is free and comfortable. Lift the head and very gently "tug" the hair or stroke the scalp from the base of the neck over the sides of the head to the crown. Do three repetitions of this movement.

SCALP MASSAGE

Place the tips of the fingers of both your hands on either side of the head, on the hairline near the temple, and using small circular motions work your fingers and thumbs toward the crown of the head 1.

Next, slide your fingers back to the hairline 2. Do three repetitions of this movement. Should you feel tension on the scalp, relieve it by concentrating specifically on that area during the massage process.

Place your palms on either side of the crown, interlock your fingers around the top of the head, and squeeze the scalp gently 3. Hold this for 30 seconds, then release the hands slowly. Next, see if you can move the skin of the scalp. Do this by holding the flat of your palms alongside the temples and making a large circular motion, thus moving a lot of the skin 4. Repeat the motion until you find the scalp relaxing.

KNUCKLE MOVEMENTS

Form your hand into a fist and spread your fingers so that there is space between them. Using the lower joints of the knuckles to move across the scalp, begin to vibrate your fingers. Start above the ears and work gently toward the top of the crown of the head. When your knuckles reach the top of the scalp, spread out your fingers down toward the ears and squeeze the head gently again. Do three repetitions of this movement.

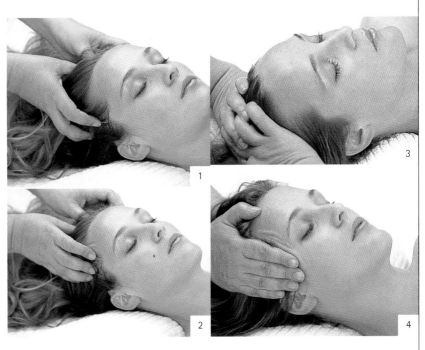

1

2

3

4

THE FACE

MASSAGING THE FACE

Apply oil to the cheeks and forehead using the palms of your hands. Put your hands on the forehead with your fingers facing each other and the palms closest to the temples.

Then pull ever so slightly toward the top of the ears, allowing your palms to lift off the forehead, but not your fingertips. Do three repetitions of this movement.

Next, feather from the chin up to the ears using only your fingertips. Now place your ring finger on each temple and allow it to rest there for a moment.

The next sequence resembles a dance and should be done keeping a clear rhythm:

1. Apply gentle pressure on the point between mouth and chin using one ring finger on top of the other.
2. Move one finger to each side of the mouth applying gentle pressure.
3. Slide your fingers to a point on either side of the nose, and press down gently.
4. Slide the fingers to a point parallel to the eyes, that is, one finger in line with the outside of each eye.
5. Bring both fingers to the center of the forehead, on the "third eye" area.
6. Slide the fingers so that they are in line with the pupils, on the forehead just above the eyebrows, and apply gentle pressure.
7. Slide your hands back to the starting point on the chin. Do three repetitions of this sequence.

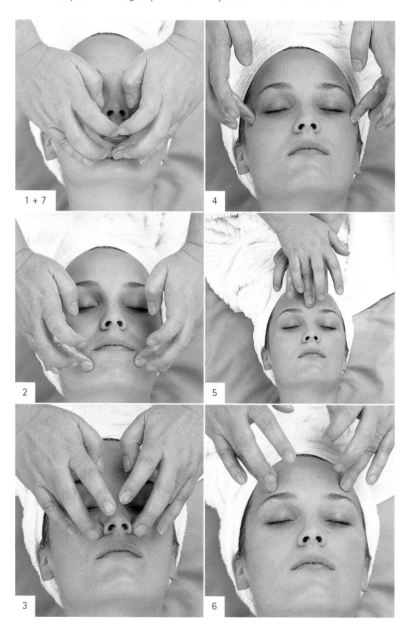

1 + 7

4

2

5

3

6

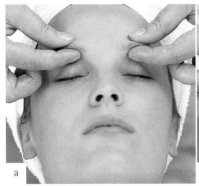
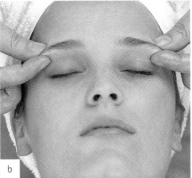
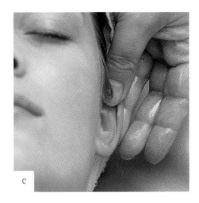

Eyebrow Pinch

The aforementioned sequence can be followed by an eyebrow "pinch." Put your thumb and forefinger over the nose edge corner of the eyebrow . Grasp the eyebrow gently and pinch it in sections until you reach the outer edge of the eyebrow . Slide your fingers back across the forehead and repeat the eyebrow pinch. On the last eyebrow pinch movement you can slide your hands toward the ears.

The Ears

Put a little oil on your fingers and with both hands gently rub the ears . Lightly pinch the outside rim of the ear from the top to the lobe, and press the ears back to the head very gently. When you have finished the ear, gently tug at the earlobe and move your hands easily down to the neck.

The Neck

Humans respond to stress much like animals do: when a cat is frightened, it will immediately arch its back; the hair on the back of a dog's neck rises; a horse will buck; and humans lift or hunch their shoulders, tensing the back and neck muscles. A neck massage can therefore release a great amount of tension.

Allow the tips of your fingers to meet at the base of the neck, and holding the weight of your partner's head in your hands, lean back very gently. This gives the neck a subtle stretch. Slide your hands down to the shoulder, so that your thumbs are on the back and your fingers are on the front of the shoulders, just touching the clavicle.

Still facing your partner's head, and with your hands on the shoulders, push down onto them, gradually applying more pressure. This is a pleasurable sensation—we are not really able to do this movement for ourselves, and seldom drop our own shoulders to this extent.

Moving to the neck, make a fist at either side of the neck and spread out your fingers, so that the middle joint on each hand is touching the skin on your partner's neck. Now rhythmically apply pressure from one finger to the next until you have covered the entire neck muscle.

Turning the Head

Open your right hand and slide it under the head, gently lift it, and turn it so that it is facing the right. Place your left hand on the shoulder and gently push down. You will see the strong tendon that supports the head on the neck. Bend your left index finger and grasp this tendon between your index finger and thumb. Gently squeeze the tendon, moving your hand up the neck toward the head. Slide your fingers back down to the shoulder and do three repetitions of this movement.

Move the head to face the left, and repeat the above sequence on the tendon on the right-hand side of the neck.

Finally, bring the head to the upward-facing position and gently make circular movements with your middle finger over the forehead. If the person being massaged has by this stage "disappeared" into a state of complete relaxation, wait until they open their eyes.

THE TORSO AND ABDOMEN

POSITION YOURSELF TO one side of the recipient. Apply oil across the abdomen and chest ☐1. Move both your hands so that they meet in the middle of the chest, and slide one hand on top of the other onto the sternum, or breast bone ☐2.

Slide your hands over the breastbone, outward along the ribs, and to the side of the body ☐3 + ☐4, making sure that the recipient's arms are slightly away from the body, then pull down the body with your fingers, using a feathering motion ☐5. Do not work too lightly. This movement is really more like pulling than feathering. If you work too lightly on the sides of the body, you

will certainly tickle; that is not what the intention is here. Do this twice and then move to the right-hand side.

Face toward the head and stand or kneel on the right side of your partner, next to the hip. Oil your hands and put them on either side of the navel, thumbs touching below the navel and index fingers touching above the navel, so that you have almost a diamond-shaped space over the navel ☐6.

> **Please note:** Many people do not like their abdomen being massaged. It is included here as an option.

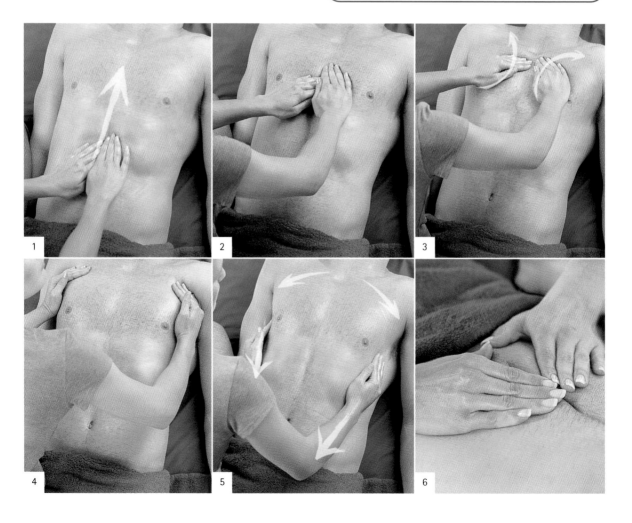

66

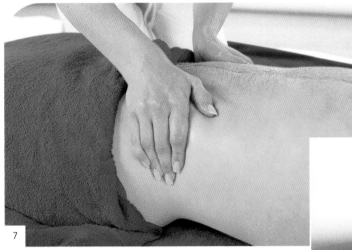

7

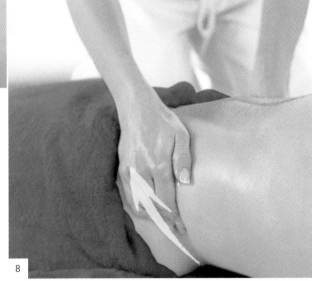

8

Slide your hands to the sides at the waist and cover the area with oil. Bring your hands back over the abdomen to the navel again; do this three times, each time lifting the skin a little more than previously, so that you can almost lift the body on the third round ⁊ + ⑧.

Glide your fingers over the stomach and make small, gentle, circular, clockwise movements with your first three fingers around the stomach area.

Bring your hands to just above the pubic bone, still on the abdomen, on the right-hand side of the body. Using both hands, trace over the colon area (just under the navel) with alternating small, circular movements, almost in a figure-of-eight shape. Keep the movement flowing and make sure your hands do not lose contact with the body.

You have just massaged the area in which the colon is situated. It is important to do this in the same direction as the colon extends, right to left, otherwise you might trap air and toxins in the colon, causing later pain or discomfort. Massage in this area is extremely relaxing, but is contraindicated in the case of a spastic colon or irritable bowel syndrome.

Do this abdominal massage three times, taking care over the bladder area—it is uncomfortable to have pressing on the bladder.

To complete the abdominal massage, add a little oil to your hands and place them on the lower abdomen, the heel of each hand just above the pubic bone, and fingers pointing toward the waist. Then very gently put a little pressure on the heels of your hands, slide them up toward the navel, and bring them down sideways over the top of the hips. Repeat the movement three times.

When you have completed the abdominal massage, ask the recipient to turn over onto his front so that you can continue with the massage sequence, focusing your attention on the legs and the back. Hold the covering towel over his body so that he does not get cold, and do not engage in conversation at this stage. The recipient should stay as relaxed as possible, as this provides the greatest benefit.

Massaging the Legs

The legs are another overworked part of the body, especially for individuals with a non-sedentary lifestyle. They are constantly supporting our body weight, and therefore benefit greatly from a good treatment session.

When you massage the legs, you essentially work against gravity, and away from the legs' natural inclination when they are upright. This novel sensation results in an effective movement of fluid through the body. A particularly good time for a leg massage is after exercise; massage will move any excess fluid from inflammation or swelling of the muscle tissue, relieving any discomfort that may have manifested itself as a result.

To begin the leg massage, move yourself to the right-hand side of your partner's body, level with the legs, placing your knees approximately in line with the recipient's knees.

The Back of the Legs

Apply oil to the feet and calves by spreading your hand over the sole of the foot and up the calf with quite firm effleurage strokes. Facing the right-hand calf, and using the flat of your hand to apply firm pressure, stroke up the leg. The little finger side of your hand should face the head, the thumb the feet, as you stroke in an upward motion toward the knee.

Lift the lower leg, support it with one hand, and do the same stroke to the crease of the knee ⬜1. Do three repetitions of this movement. Lower the leg and glide up the thigh toward the buttock. Slide your hand back down on the sides of the thigh with a feathering movement.

Massaging the Calves

Grip the calf quite firmly between your thumbs and fingers and pull the muscle gently upward, away from the bone. Repeat this with the other hand and so establish a rhythm going up the leg to the knee, then slide down to the ankle again and knead up the calf and back down again a few times.

After kneading the calf muscle find a "seam" directly along the Achilles tendon area in the middle of the calf muscle, where a stocking seam would be. Using the tips of your fingers glide up this stocking seam ⬜2, using one hand immediately after the other, creating a continuous rhythm all the way up the leg to the buttock. Gently press into the point at the crease of the buttock and return to the foot, using your fingers to feather down the sides of the leg ⬜3. Do three repetitions of this movement.

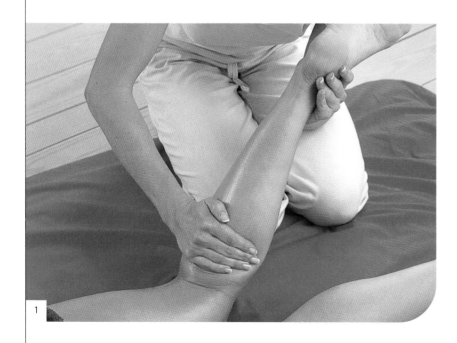

1

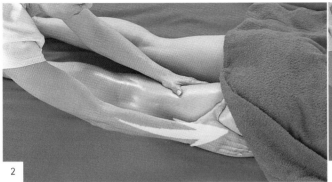

2

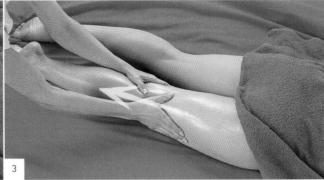

3

Leg Slides

Face your thumbs toward each other, along the center "seam" of the calf. The fingers should face the towel on the floor. Slide your hands over the calf moving upward to the crease at the back of the knee; lighten the pressure as you slide your hands behind the knee, and as you come to the thigh where the leg thickens, spread your hands apart and carry on gliding up the leg. When you reach the top of the leg, spread your fingers slightly apart and feather down the sides of the leg again.

Do three repetitions of this movement. This action assists in lymphatic drainage by moving fluid toward the lymphatic nodes behind the knees and at the top of the leg. Due to increased circulation, toxins are then removed from the body.

Wringing over the Leg

Using your whole hand, grasp the muscle and wring, pushing the muscle with one hand and pulling it with the other a. Work all the way up the leg in this manner, then feather down toward the feet again.

Kneading

Grasp the calf muscle with your hands and, alternating rhythmically with each hand, gently squeeze: left-hand squeeze, release; right-hand squeeze, release b. Work over the calf first, then up the outside of the thigh, and then along the inside of the thigh, starting above the knee.

For a smooth transition to the back, do a gentle effleurage movement on the leg before moving up to the back.

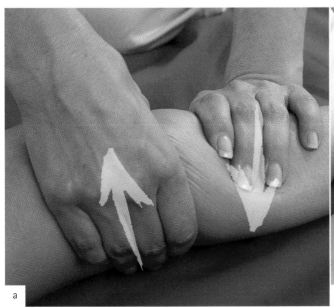

a

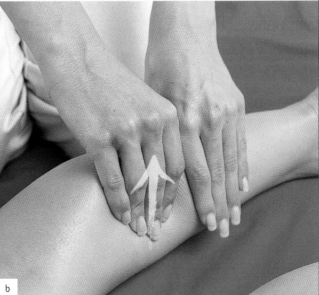

b

THE BACK

THE BACK ROUTINE is very important in a massage, as most of our stress is stored in the back muscles. Of the 12 major muscle groups located in the back, the trapezius muscle and the *latissimus dorsi* probably work the hardest. The trapezius, which covers the back and shoulders, is used in standing, sitting, and nearly every movement of the body.

The *latissimus dorsi* is the largest muscle in the back, and extends from the armpit to the lower back. It is this muscle that often causes people lower backache and, to the surprise of many, a shoulder massage can often help treat pain in this area. Should you have a limited amount of time, then a back massage is the best you can offer.

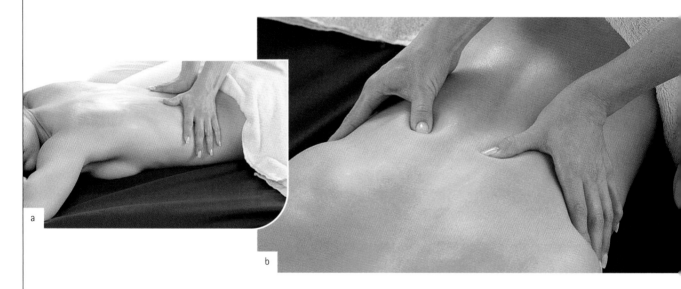

a

b

APPLYING OIL

Put oil in your palms and then place the flats of your hands on the recipient's lower back [a]. Remember that the oil is to be applied onto the recipient; avoid the inclination to spread the oil onto your own hands. With the heel of each hand near the spine, allow your hands to glide up the back and over the shoulders, then slide the whole hand down on your return to the lower back. Repeat these effleurage movements until the entire back is covered in oil.

Change the position of the hands; turn them so that the fingers face the spine. Repeat the above sequence, adding more oil at this stage if you feel it is necessary.

THUMB CRAWLING ON THE BACK

Change the position of your fingers so that your thumbs are facing each other, resting against the vertebrae. Establish a rhythm as you slide your thumbs up either side of the spine [b]. Slide, pause, allow the other thumb to slide, meet the first thumb, slide the first thumb, pause, allow the other thumb to slide up to meet it—do all this in a rhythm and you will immediately relax the recipient.

Do this stroke up either side of the spine, first on the right-hand side, then on the left. Repeat the whole sequence slowly and rhythmically three times. If you know the recipient is really enjoying it, you can repeat this as often as you like.

CIRCLING ON THE BACK

With your hands on either side of the spine, but about 2in (5cm) away from it, and again using your thumbs, massage from the lower back toward the shoulders [1]. You can rotate the thumbs—the left one anticlockwise and the right one clockwise. Slide up slowly and then glide your hands, using a feathering movement, back to the base of the spine. Repeat this three times. When you reach the shoulders pay special attention to the tight muscle at the top of the shoulders, as this needs to be worked on quite firmly.

LONG THUMB SLIDES

Using the soft thumb pads, slide up the muscles next to the spine [2] till you reach the shoulders, then pull down with all your fingers toward the lower back until your hands come to rest at the base of the spine. Repeat this stroke, making sure to work the muscles on both side of the spine. Once you have worked these muscles a few times using alternate thumbs, you will have located any areas of tension.

MASSAGING OVER AREAS OF TENSION

When you feel a specific area is very tense, massage it using both your thumbs and firm stroking movements. Press down with your thumb and maintain the pressure, stroking as far as the length of your own thumb, making small concentrated strokes and always moving in the same direction as the muscle fiber, from the lower back toward the shoulders.

FLAT HAND FANNING

Spread out one hand, starting at the lower back with the heel of your hand resting on the muscle next to the spine. Slide your hand in a semicircular motion from the side of the spine to the side of the body. Let the other hand do the next gliding movement, so that the pattern of massage looks like two fans lying next to one another [3], and cover the whole back with this movement.

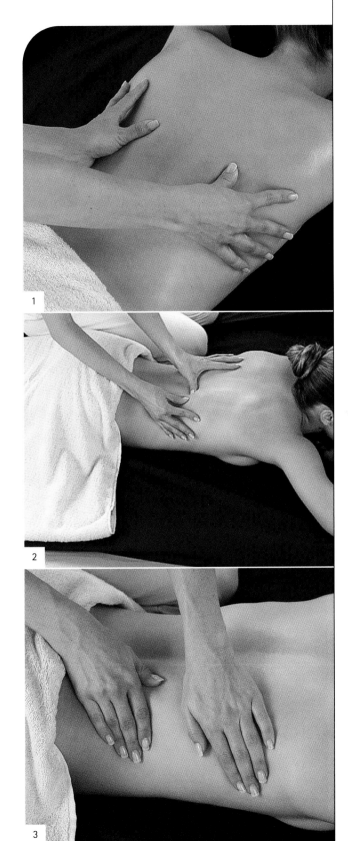

ENDING THE MASSAGE

At the end of a massage the recipient will be completely relaxed—and it is important to "ground" him or her. This is done by allowing your hands to hover over the body's energy field and stroking the energy down to the feet.

This is done with a gentle, brushing movement from head to foot, keeping your hands just above and not touching the body. To complete the massage, hold the ankles firmly but gently for a few moments.

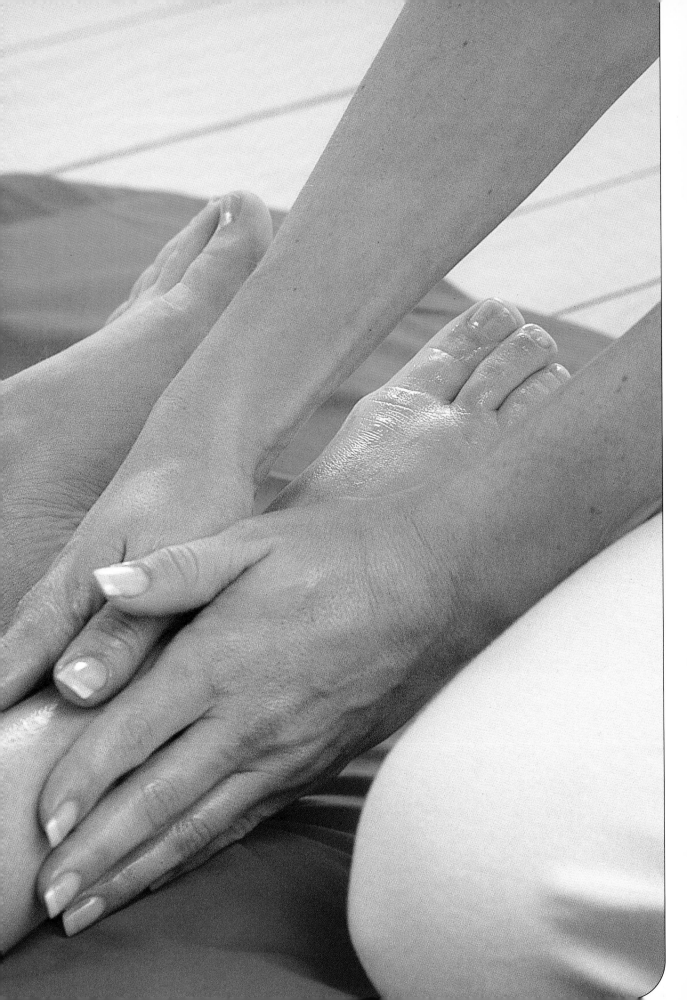

THERE ARE certain circumstances in life that will require a different approach to massage, as well as situations where massage will be even more appreciated, such as massaging pregnant women or the elderly.

Pregnancy is one of the most special times in a woman's life—it is also one of the most physically challenging. Massage is an excellent way to relieve some of the symptoms associated with pregnancy, such as lower back pain.

A parent who massages a baby not only relaxes the child but offers one of the most basic and physical manifestations of love. This can be extended to the elderly, as we often forget that our parents need touch as much as our children.

Finally, after spending time on others, turn attention on yourself with a relaxing self-massage routine.

Right A parent's tender massage will allow the infant to become familiar with its body through the sensation of touch.

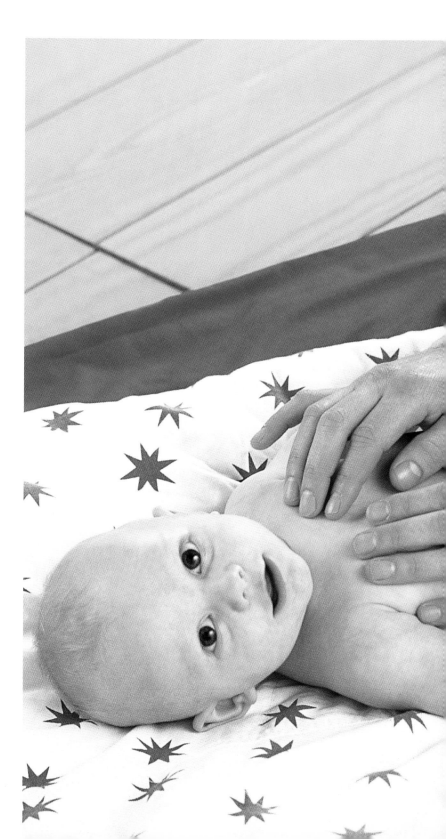

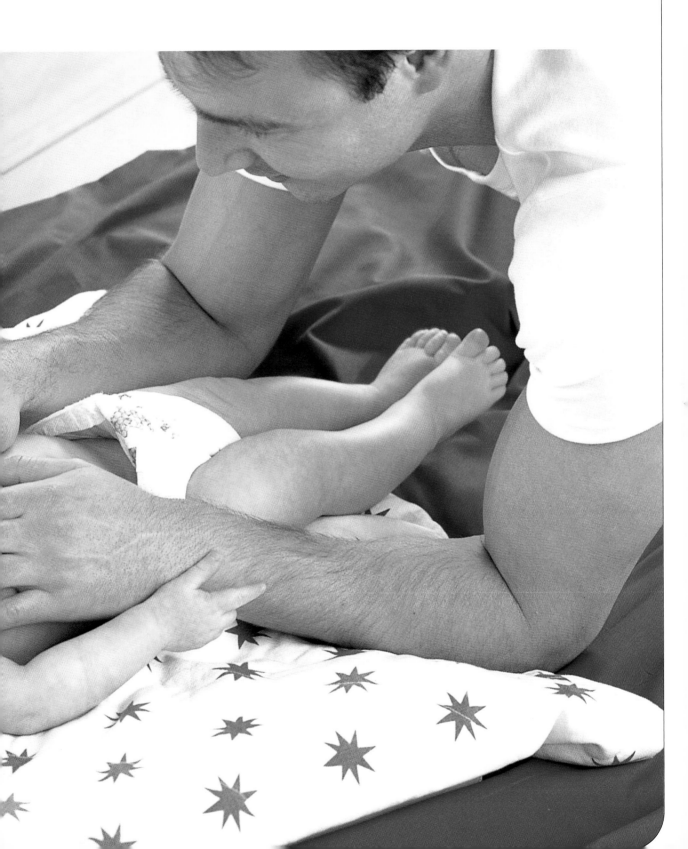

MASSAGE DURING PREGNANCY

THE TYPE AND intensity of the massage given during pregnancy depends on the stage to which the pregnancy has advanced. If the recipient can still lie on her front, you can follow the same sequence as in normal massage routines.

Be very careful about using essential oils. These oils are the essences of medicinal plants and some can be abortifacients, or can bring on menstruation. **Do NOT** use oils such as wintergreen or pennyroyal, as these may affect the fetus if used in large amounts.

Err on the side of caution and only use mandarin or Neroli essential oils during pregnancy. The advantage in using Neroli is that it helps to prevent stretch marks.

THE MASSAGE ROUTINE

Have your partner lie on her back with a cushion under her knees, so that there is no strain on the lower back. Gently apply oil and then massage her feet and ankles—these may often be swollen, as many women carry extra water during their pregnancy. Do not use any pressure points, as this is contraindicated in pregnancy.

Follow the arm massage sequence discussed on p61, as well as the head and shoulder sequence on p63 and p73, respectively. When you have completed these movements, arrange for your partner to lie on her side with a cushion between her knees or sit on a chair "back to front" so that she can lean her arms on the backrest of the chair.

If the woman chooses to sit on a chair, you will not be able work on the legs, so start with the back. You may find it easier to sit on a stool at this stage.

Tips for Massaging during Pregnancy:

☐ Use gentle effleurage strokes with calming and soothing movements.

☐ If your relationship with the recipient allows, massage around the abdomen in a circular motion.

☐ **Do NOT** under any circumstances use heavy petrissage movements and tapotement, as these overstimulate the body and counteract the calming effect of massage.

☐ Realize that the hormone balance is different during pregnancy and that you are dealing with another little being as well as the mother.

☐ Always maintain a positive and happy disposition.

BACK MASSAGE

During her pregnancy, a woman often has more strain than normal on her trapezius muscle, which extends across the back and shoulders. Her breasts are usually heavier, and she is also likely to be carrying additional weight. A pregnant woman's back muscles will certainly take more strain, and massaging up the trapezius toward the neck and shoulders is an important part of pregnancy massage.

Start the massage approximately at the waistline 1; using circular thumb motions, move up the outer edge of the trapezius. Next, using thumb slides and applying a little pressure, slide up the trapezius muscle with the thumb, apply a little pressure, then slide, establishing a rhythm. Maintain it until you reach the top of the shoulders.

Move your thumbs to either side of the spine, thumb crawl up the spine, and repeat this three times 2. Then spread your hands and fan slide from the lower back up to the shoulders: with the heel of your hand facing the lower back and your fingers facing her shoulder, allow your fingers to slide in semicircles like windscreen wipers, one hand after the other in a fanning movement 3, so as to cover the whole back. Note that in the fanning movement the fingers are supple and not held rigid, thus increasing the effect of this movement.

a

Stand up behind your partner and gently massage her shoulders with your thumbs, kneading the muscles on top of and around her shoulder blades a. Work in circular thumb motions around the shoulder blades and be conscious of the fact that you may find tight muscles in this area. If you do, continue to work on them until they relax.

Slide your hands up to the neck for the next stage of the massage. Using your right index finger and thumb, squeeze gently up the neck from the back to the base of the skull. Slowly spread the index finger and thumb apart, applying a little pressure to relieve tension.

End the sequence with a scalp massage, doing gentle circles with your fingers over the whole scalp. There is a very good chance that at this stage your partner will want to go to sleep!

1

2

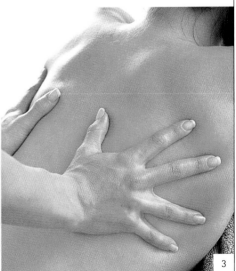

3

MASSAGING BABIES

BABY MASSAGE HAS become very popular in recent years. Warming and stroking movements will not only remind the baby of its secure and protected environment in the womb; psychologists specializing in early childhood development have discovered that when a child is made to feel secure through touch, there is a speeding up of nerve growth, increased cellular activity, and endocrine gland function.

Playing with an infant's toes and fingers, rubbing its back and neck—these are all pleasurable sensations that allow the infant to experience its body through the sensation of touch. Being touched is the baby's first real experience of love, and we can enhance all aspects of an infant's well-being by giving him or her a massage. A parent who massages a baby is doing much more for that child than any material gift could ever do.

THE CORRECT ENVIRONMENT

You may enjoy being massaged outdoors, in the sun, but infants will probably feel more secure in their own room or in a secure room that is neither too draughty nor too bright. Infants are very sensitive to sound, so you should choose a quiet place that is devoid of people talking and loud noises. The room should be warm and preferably dimly lit to promote relax-

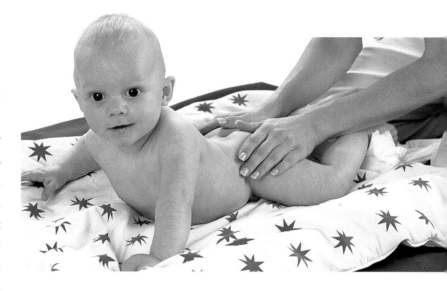

ation. You may wish to play soft music and will quickly be able to gauge which music your baby responds to best.

If you want to massage your baby while sitting on the floor, put down a flat baby mattress that will make it comfortable for both of you. Cover the cushion or baby mattress with a plastic cover and have a nappy or diaper at hand. One has to be prepared for any eventuality with infants, especially when they are relaxed!

Be self-assured when massaging your baby, as tentative strokes will make him or her feel insecure. Babies need to receive the message via your hands that you know what you are doing, so that they can build up faith in you for life.

OILS

Do not use essential oils when massaging small infants, as their livers are tiny and cannot process the oil that is absorbed through the skin. A small amount of baby oil is recommended.

Try to carry out baby massage at floor level, as the oil used will make the baby slippery and difficult to hold or grasp. If you are massaging your baby on the dining room table, make sure that it is secured all the way around the edge by the use of rolled up towels or cushions.

It is best to massage midway between feeds—a hungry baby is going to want food instead of a massage, and a baby who has just eaten is likely to throw up during the massage.

THE MASSAGE ROUTINE

With the baby lying on its back, apply a little oil with your hand. Make a stroke from the infant's right hip across and up to the left shoulder 1. Repeat this with your other hand across the little body from left hip to right shoulder.

Bring both your hands down across the top of the leg to the foot. Take one foot quite firmly in your hand and use your thumb to massage under the foot in tiny circular movements 2. Do not tickle! As tempting as it may be to have the child giggle, this is not what you are aiming for in this massage sequence.

Take two of your fingers and gently play with your baby's toes; then give the little legs a gentle squeeze right up to the top of the leg. The first squeeze will be at the back of the leg at the Achilles tendon, and you should only use your thumb and forefinger for this 3; use your whole hand when you reach the calf muscle. Keep squeezing gently to the top of the leg.

Slide your hand down the side of the leg and start again at the Achilles tendon, working up the leg. Repeat this three times. Change your hands and massage the other leg in the same way.

Get your baby to lie as still as you can. Stroke up from the pubic bone with your right hand for a hand's width, then start again with the other hand, a little higher on the body. Do the next stroke, move a little higher, change hands for the next stroke—continue until you have established a rhythm. Carry on right up over the chest to the shoulder. Return to the top of the pubic bone by reversing the stroke that you have done, now working down from the shoulders.

Moving to the arms, gently squeeze them in the same way as you did the legs; then play with the fingers. Spend time on each individual finger and, while you are doing this, use your index finger to stroke the palm of your little one's hand.

Having done the arms, turn the baby over onto its front, making sure that it is comfortable and can breathe easily. Apply a little olive oil to the buttocks, then smooth your hand from the outside of the thigh over the entire buttock area. Repeat this three times, then slide your hands up the back and, keeping your fingers next to the spine, slowly stroke downward. Repeat this a few times, then stroke the baby from the shoulders right down to the soles of the feet. You can end the massage by giving the baby a few gentle pats on the buttock.

Baby massage is something that the father of the child should be encouraged to do. It is one of the greatest bonding mechanisms we have, and the father will experience a closeness to the child that is quite different from merely holding it.

MASSAGING THE AGED

AGING IS A natural process, which unfortunately reduces some of our physical functions. As exercise is cut out of our routine, more of our natural functions are reduced—our metabolism slows down and it becomes more difficult to do physical work without slowing down to catch our breath; the arteries are not as resilient anymore, and some elderly folk suffer from osteoporosis, while many have chronic disorders.

Many elderly people are only rarely touched by another person at this time of their lives. Imagine what it is like to live alone and not to be touched and nurtured. Regrettably this is commonplace with the elderly around the world. Elderly people really appreciate and benefit both mentally and physically from a massage. Most regard a massage as a special treat.

PRECAUTIONS

If there is any sign of osteoporosis, or brittle bones, err on the side of caution over bony areas—just one over-firm massage stroke can crack a rib. The skin may be paper-thin, so do use sufficient oil to ensure good lubrication. In the case of very dry skin, add two capsules of vitamin A oil to the massage oil—this will feed the skin in addition to providing lubrication.

When massaging the elderly you use the same techniques applied in normal massage—except for knuckling and deep tissue massage—but there are certain changes necessary to deal with the circumstances of age. One of these is pressure. Use far less pressure than you would on a younger person. A little friction is acceptable as it encourages the circulation,

but be careful about doing any friction strokes over sensitive or dry skin. In general you need to be very gentle with the elderly, as their skin tends to bruise easily.

If you offer a massage to an elderly person, bear in mind that it may be a new experience, and he or she may be reluctant to accept as he/she is unsure what to expect. A good approach is to start by offering a foot massage—once they have experienced this it is inevitable they will ask for more!

FOOT MASSAGE

Sit opposite the recipient on a chair lower than hers and rest the heel of her bare foot on a towel on your knee. Take the right foot in your hands and hold it for a few moments, then begin gently molding the foot with your hands, so that the recipient becomes used to your touch.

Have a small bottle of oil ready and spread this over the top of the foot with the palm of your hand. Apply oil to the sole of the foot, too.

Put your hands on both sides of the foot, cupping the ankle in your palms, and let your fingers face

1

2

3

the Achilles tendon at the back of the heel. Wiggle your hands back and forth quite quickly, so that the ankle moves from side to side between your palms. This may not be easy at first, but it is worth practicing as there is a lot of energy stored in the ankle. The recipient will often want to be in control of the wiggling—let them know tactfully that this is not the idea.

Next, take the foot firmly in your right hand and, holding it over the area of the arch, rotate the foot gently. This is another exercise that your partner might want to "help" you with.

Now with your thumbs on the top of the foot and your fingers on the sole, rub the sole of the foot from the heel to the toes in a circular motion ①.

Change your hands so that your thumbs are on the soles, your palms on the top of the foot. Using the caterpillar crawl, work your thumbs from the outside edge of the foot across the ball of the foot, then return by working from the inside edge of the foot to the outer edge ② + ③, and all the way from the ball of the foot to the heel. You may feel that some areas of the foot are more sensitive than others—work across the sensitive areas until the sensation changes.

Go back to the top of the foot and work down the valleys of the toes as described on p56. Having done that, you will probably need to add more oil to your hands before attempting the next stroke.

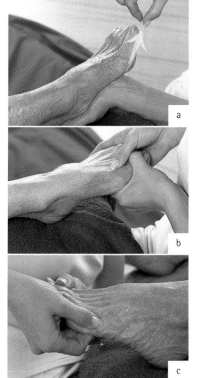

a

b

c

Slide one of your hands, palm side down, over the ankle, and repeat this at least three times. Then lightly pinch each toe. Squeeze from the base of the toe to the tip, then flick your fingers in the air to remove any negative energy from your hands a . When you come to the big toe, rotate it gently and then repeat this rotation with every toe. In reflexology the toes represent the head, and rotating the toes relaxes the neck, which we have previously described as an area in which stress is held.

Next, rub along the top of the foot from the toes to the ankle with small circular movements using both thumbs b . Begin between the big toe and the second toe, and circle all the way to the ankle, then glide your fingers back to the indentation between the next two toes. Continue this process until you reach the edge of the little toe. To end this movement, pinch down the outside of the foot from the little toe to the heel c .

Go back to the movement in which you wiggled the foot by holding the ankles between your palms; then, to complete the foot massage, feather down the foot lightly with the tips of your fingers, gently bringing the energy down to the toes.

Cover the feet with a towel or have the recipient put on socks to keep the feet warm, and to prevent slipping as a result of the oil on the feet. This is a suitable massage to give at night as it induces sleep.

Reflexology is a gentle, noninvasive treatment that can offer a number of benefits. If the treatment is not required to focus on a particular area of discomfort, it can take the form of a relaxing massage and assist the body to rid itself of toxins and emotional debris.

AYURVEDIC MASSAGE

Ayurveda is the ancient Indian "science of life"—a completely natural way of obtaining health, harmony, and happiness. Ayurvedic principles are known to have influenced the development of Chinese, Arabic, Greek, and Roman medicine and, more recently, Western medicine has also adopted Ayurvedic concepts and therapies.

Ayurvedic massage works on both a physical and mental level, transmitting an energy that assists the body and its organs to repair and renew themselves. Practitioners concentrate on subtle energy points on the body that respond to gentle physical manipulation, and work with the needs of different body types.

Ayurvedic massage is normally carried out as part of an Ayurvedic cleansing process known as Pancha karma (five actions). During this process, warm herbal oil is lavished on the body using special techniques

for various conditions, which can include: rheumatism, nervous complaints, anxiety- and stress-related conditions, low blood pressure, and diseases of the immune system.

Having mastered the massage techniques outlined in this book, you may wish to take an interest in other forms of massage. If so, either contact a practitioner or institution in your area, or one of the associations or organizations listed on p94.

THAI MASSAGE

This ancient therapeutic procedure has its roots in Indian Ayurvedic medicine and yoga. Traditional Thai massage fluidly blends gentle rocking, rhythmic acupressure, and assisted stretches to relax and revitalize body and mind.

The body's energy lines are the focus of Thai massage. Although similar to the meridians of Chinese acupressure, Thai energy lines, known as Sen, flow through the entire body and are not associated with specific organs. The masseuse exerts pressure on the energy lines and pressure points along them, using the palms, thumbs, feet, and occasionally elbows. Pressure therapy is combined with passive stretching movements that relax the body, releasing tension and increasing flexibility.

Right **Thai massage is readily enjoyed by many a visitor to the country, often in idyllic settings such as this one on the island of Koh Tao.**

USEFUL CONTACTS

For information on massage therapists in your area, try the Yellow Pages or the societies and associations listed below.

U.S.A. AND CANADA

IMA GROUP, INTERNATIONAL MASSAGE ASSOCIATION, INC.
- P.O. Drawer 421
  Warrenton, VA 20188–0421
  U.S.A.
- Tel: (540) 351-0800
- Fax: (540) 351-0816
- email: info@imagroup.com
- www.imagroup.com

AMERICAN MASSAGE THERAPY ASSOCIATION
- 820 Davis Street, Suite 100
  Evanston, IL 60201–4444
  U.S.A.
- Tel: (847) 864-0123
- Fax: (847) 864-1178
- www.amtamassage.org

CMTA, CANADIAN MASSAGE THERAPIST ALLIANCE
- 365 Bloor Street East, Suite 1807
  Toronto, Ontario M4W 3L4
  Canada
- Tel: (416) 968-2149
- Fax: (416) 968-6818
- www.cmta.ca

UK AND IRELAND

GENERAL COUNCIL FOR MASSAGE THERAPY
- 46 Millmead Way
  Hertford SG14 3YH
  United Kingdom
- Tel: +44 (1992) 537-637
- email: admin@gcmt-uk.org

BMTC, BRITISH MASSAGE THERAPY COUNCIL
- 17 Rymers Lane
  Oxon OX4 3JU
  United Kingdom
- Tel/Fax: +44 (1865) 774-123
- email: info@bmtc.co.uk
- www.bmtc.co.uk

THE BRITISH REFLEXOLOGY ASSOCIATION
- Monks Orchard
  Whitbourne WR6 5RB
  United Kingdom
- Tel: +44 (1886) 821-207
- Fax: +44 (1886) 822-017
- email: bra@britreflex.co.uk
- www.britreflex.co.uk

EUROPE

AXELSONS INSTITUTE
- Gästrikegatan 10
  11382 Stockholm
  Sweden
- Tel: +46 (8) 54-54-59-00
- Fax: +46 (8) 341-152
- email: info@axelsons.se
- www.axelsons.se

AUSTRALIA

MASSAGE AUSTRALIA
- P.O. Box 13
  Windang, NSW 2528
- Tel: +61 (2) 4295-7720
- Fax: +61 (2) 4295-7898
- email: info@massageaus.com.au
- www.massageaus.com.au

AMTA, ASSOCIATION OF MASSAGE THERAPISTS AUSTRALIA
- P.O. Box 358
  Prahran, Victoria 3181
- Tel: +61 (3) 9510-3930
- Fax: +61 (3) 9521-3209
- email: amta@amta.asn.au
- www.amta.asn.au

NEW ZEALAND

TMA, THERAPEUTIC MASSAGE ASSOCIATION
- P.O. Box 29-219, Greenwoods Corner
  Auckland
- Tel: +64 (9) 623-8269
- Fax: +64 (9) 623-8260
- email: info@nzatmp.org.nz
- www.nzatmp.org.nz

SOUTH AFRICA

MASSAGE THERAPY ASSOCIATION
- P.O. Box 53320
  Kenilworth 7745
  Cape Town
- Tel: +27 (21) 671-5313
- email: swilliams@ntasa.co.za

INDEX

BIBLIOGRAPHY AND FURTHER READING

Smith, K. (1999) *Massage The Healing Power of Touch.* London: Duncan Baird Publishers.

Mitchell, S. (1997) *The Complete Illustrated Guide to Massage.* Shaftesbury: Element Books Limited.

Malik, S. (1996) *Massage for Health and Healing.* New Delhi: Abhinav Publications.

Maxwell-Hudson, C. (1988) *The Complete Book of Massage.* London: Dorling Kindersley.

Johari, H. (1996) *Ayurvedic Massage—Traditional Indian Techniques for Balancing Body and Mind.* Healing Arts Press.

Swami Sada Shiva Tirtha. *The Ayurveda Encyclopedia.* AHD Press.

Rand, W. (1991) *Reiki, The Healing Touch.* Southfield: Vision Publications.

Lundberg, P. (1992) *The Book of Shiatsu.* London: Gaia Books.

Dougans, I. (1996) *The Complete Illustrated Guide to Reflexology.* London: Element Books.

Gillanders, A. *The Essential Guide to Foot and Hand Reflexology.* London: Gaia Books.

Ranger, H. (2001) *Everybody's Aromatherapy—a comprehensive guide for all ages.* Cape Town: Tafelberg.

Marieb, E. (1995) *Anatomy and Physiology.* Redwood City: The Benjamin/Cummings Publishing Company Inc.

PICTURE CREDITS

All photography by Neil Hermann, with the exception of those supplied by the following photographers and/or agencies (copyright rests with these individuals and/or their agencies):

Endpapers....Photo Access/Justin Pumfrey

1 ....Photo Access/Justin Pumfrey

2-3 ....Gallo Images/Christopher Thomas

4-5 ....Photo Access

8-9.................Hutchison Library

10-11 ....British Library

12 ....Fotozone

13 ....Werner Foreman Archive

14 ....Hulton Getty/Gallo Images

15....................Image Bank

18...................Photonica/Elke Hesser

24...................Gallo Images

88-89 ....Gallo Images

90...................Photo Access

91 ....Susan Crawshaw

92-93 ....Travel Ink/Colin Marshall

ACKNOWLEDGMENTS

Models: Tasmin, Charine, Dave Horne, Amelia, Lucy, Eleanor.

Make Up: Robyn Nissen. Styling: Sasha Lee Walton.

Clothing supplied by Claudine of Namaste Yoga and Exercise Wear